RULING OVER
MONARCHS,
GIANTS & STARS

UMPIRING IN THE NEGRO LEAGUES
& BEYOND

BOB MOTLEY
WITH BYRON MOTLEY

SP
SPORTS
PUBLISHING
L.L.C.

SportsPublishingLLC.com

Author photo by Richard Lotman Brown. All additional photos courtesy of Bob Motley unless otherwise noted.

Publishers: Peter L. Bannon and Joseph J. Bannon Sr.
Senior managing editor: Susan M. Moyer
Editor: Doug Hoepker
Art director and cover design: K. Jeffrey Higgerson
Photo editor: Erin Linden-Levy

Sports Publishing L.L.C.
804 North Neil Street
Champaign, IL 61820

Library of Congress Cataloging-in-Publication Data available upon request.
ISBN: 978-1-59670-236-3

Printed in the United States of America

For my wife, Pearline

No words can adequately express the love and appreciation
I have for you, or the daily joy I experience in sharing my
life with you. You are my partner, best friend, and greatest
love all wrapped into one. Our lives together these past 55
years have been more than spectacular.
We have been well blessed.

"This shall be written for the generation to come."
—*Psalm 102:18*

CONTENTS

FOREWORD

By Larry Lester

IT WAS THE EARLY 1990s in Kansas City, home of barbeque and blues, that I met Robert "Bob" Motley at a meeting of historians, politicians, community leaders, and former players to discuss the formation of a museum that would showcase the times, the travels, and the experiences of the Negro Baseball Leagues. As a researcher and historian, I was familiar with some background information about this former Negro League umpire from various newspaper accounts and player interviews. However, until this testimonial, I never knew the extent of this modest man's extraordinary life accomplishments. I had known of his rank as a chief umpire and arbiter at a few East-West All-Star games, but little else.

Ruling over Monarchs, Giants & Stars chronicles the life and times of a "blind" umpire from Alabama's red clay country to Anniston's Buttermilk Road, to Dayton, Ohio, before landing in Monarch country, Kansas City, Missouri, in vibrant and candid detail.

In the years to come, as co-founders of the Negro Leagues Baseball Museum, I, along with fellow board members, found this warm and genuine man to be the consummate professional, a man of honor and a man of his word, as well as having a commitment to providing a high quality of life for family.

Fatherless at four, the son of a sharecropper and a stern God-fearing mama, Bob Motley was influenced by a big-boned teacher, Ms. Rowe; a grocery storeowner, Locker Burns; a hotel hustler, George Cannon; and big sis, Geraldine; to escape his preordained destiny of an impoverished life.

Readers will find Motley's memoir is more than a baseball story; it is the social history of a young man's struggle to reach his dream of umpiring at the Show, during this country's socially retarded Jim Crow period of the 1930s and '40s. Read about the influence of Jackie Robinson's triumphant travel into lily-white baseball that encouraged young Motley to complete his high school education at age 24, ultimately providing the foundation and inspiration for a productive adulthood. Learn about this Marine's brush with death, ultimately earning him a Purple Heart; his encounters with the Klan; his persistence to become a Man in Blue; and his passionate devotion to his wheelchair-bound wife, Pearline, of more than 50 years.

Motley shares with insight and humor, the engaging personalities of Leroy "Satchel" Paige, Frank Duncan, John "Buck" O'Neil, Wilber "Bullet" Rogan, Hank Aaron, Ernie Banks, Willie Mays, and Willard "Home Run" Brown ("the best ever . . ."), along with vivid images of the three diamond ladies—Toni Stone, Connie Morgan, and Mamie Johnson. This is an insider's account of what really happened between the white foul lines, in the clubhouse, and on long bus trips. Your eyes will be surprised at stories so contagious they will make you want to turn the pages.

Additionally, you will find untold stories about the energetic Albert "Buster" Haywood (Aaron's first professional manager with the Indianapolis Clowns), Negro League stars like Reece "Goose" Tatum, team owner Ted Rasberry, and a host of unheralded legends of this dark sports chapter in American life.

Ruling Over Monarchs, Giants & Stars is the legacy of a proud man who overcame adversity, and had the audacity to rise to the pinnacle of every profession he encountered, from bellboy, to military officer, to a General Motors supervisor, to chief umpire of black baseball's top professionals.

Fortunately, my father, former Negro League players, and one "blind" umpire have been great role models for me, making me proud to be a part of this new inspirational chapter in America's black history.

FOREWORD
By Dionne Warwick

HOW LUCKY WE ARE to have the pleasure of sharing in the life of this most accomplished and incredible man, Bob Motley. I am honored to have been asked to write this brief foreword to this wonderful memoir. I say brief only because the foreword would be as long as the book to say all that I would want to say.

Having had the pleasure of meeting Mr. Motley and being acquainted with him and his family for over 30 years has enriched my life. By his example, he has time and again shown what it means to be a loving and caring family man.

Growing up in New Jersey around several of the Newark Eagles' Negro League players like Monte Irvin, Don Newcombe, and Larry Doby, who all were friends of my dad, gives me a little insight into what Mr. Motley has accomplished. Becoming one of the first umpires of our race to cross the color line into organized baseball gave us another inspiring role model, a reminder that we can all strive for greatness and achieve our goals. And, may I add, with his achievement, the bar was set high for all umpires to rise to.

Becoming the best at whatever he attempted was his goal, and it's apparent this is still his personal mantra.

I know you will enjoy the journey you are about to embark upon, so ... *Enjoy!*

PREFACE
By Byron Motley

I AM THE SON OF A LIVING LEGEND. Not everyone can say that.

For a long while, I didn't say it, either. It took me many adult years before I realized or even appreciated my lineage, but I'm glad I finally came to my senses and recognized this remarkable man, Bob Motley, and his generation—which represents a significant period of our history.

My father has lived a life! You will no doubt discover that within these pages. During his formative years growing up in the segregated South, he endured the hardships of poverty and the dangers of Ku Klux Klan violence. After World War II began, he voluntarily signed up for military service, risking his life for a country that offered only limited freedoms to Negroes. Coming home from war as a decorated veteran, he and thousands of other black service men continued to be treated like second-class citizens in their own country. These incredibly brave men were still restricted from certain jobs, educational opportunities, places they could live, establishments they could enter, water fountains from which they could drink, levels of sports they could aspire to, and the right to vote. Nevertheless, being who they were, these men, my father among them, forged ahead with lofty dreams.

The dream my father held was borne out of his love for umpiring. It led him to the Negro Baseball League, where he worked as a devoted arbiter for a decade. I can personally attest to my father's amazing talents as an umpire, as I was an eyewitness to his extraordinary skill many times throughout my childhood. I was born too late to see him work in the Negro Leagues; but I did accompany my father to Ban Johnson League and college games that he umpired around my hometown of Kansas City, Missouri. I was sometimes embarrassed by the outrageous way in which he called plays, because he was so loud and animated. Many times

I purposely played with other kids, far away from the diamond, out of sight. A lot of good that did! Even when I was in an entirely different section of the park, swinging on the monkey bars, playing hide and seek, or just throwing rocks to lull away the time, I could still hear my dad's voice intermittently echoing in the distance as he called balls and strikes.

Despite my initial embarrassment, I was always impressed that many people who attended those games not only came to see the up-and-coming athletes, but also to see "that outrageous ump." Spectators loved his colorful style.

It wasn't long before my feeling of embarrassment became one of astonishment. As I grew older, I began to appreciate and accept my father for the individual he was—just like the many fans Dad had eating out of the palm of his hand had already done. He became a star in my eyes. Sometimes I'd secretly mimic him in the backyard, on playgrounds, or in the privacy of my own room.

In today's celebrity-driven market, Bob Motley could have been a star amongst the men in blue. His flamboyant style on the ball diamond could have caught the eye of some innovative marketing director and landed him an endorsement deal. Alas, like many of the Negro League celebrities of his day, my father was ahead of his time.

In addition to his prowess as a pro sports arbiter, my father has also been—and continues to be—a marvelous and engaging storyteller. I mention this gift because without it this book would not exist, nor would I had been inspired to become the historian that I am today. I distinctly remember my father reminiscing about his harrowing World War II experiences and his days in the Negro Leagues. Invariably, my mother, sister, and I would look at each other, roll our eyes and smirk as if to say, "Oh no, here he goes again!" But then, as if hearing the story for the first time, we would be mesmerized by every detail. I didn't know it then, but he was teaching me the importance of remembering our past.

As common as Daddy's stories were in our household, I figured everyone knew about the Negro Leagues. Not until my middle school years did I realize that this was far from true. The history of America's black league was not taught in school; nor was it talked about in the community. Therefore, I could not fully appreciate its impact on my life or African-American history until years later.

A man with boundless energy, my dad was an active father. He was on hand for *every* one of my piano recitals, school plays, and football, basketball, and baseball games. I was thrilled he was in the stands to witness the day I hit my one and only home run to deep center field in an eighth grade baseball game. My proudest baseball moment became even more special when he proclaimed me to be "the hero of the day!" I'll never forget that. He obviously won't forget it either, as to this very day he loves teasing me about taking "about an hour" to round the bases, basking in the afterglow of my monumental, once-in-a-lifetime achievement.

A stern disciplinarian, my father made sure my sister and I stayed on the straight and narrow path. Although we'd sometimes stray a little off course, especially during our teen years, he and my mother were always there to support, guide, direct, and counsel, all with unconditional parental love. In fact, many of my friends wanted to "adopt" my parents because they were so involved in every activity that my sister and I undertook.

When I did get into trouble I didn't like him much, but deep inside I knew that the persistent advice and discipline was for my own good. When I started to see some of my peers running amuck with no direction and little to no self-respect, I began to appreciate that fatherly wisdom and authority that he provided.

To give you an insight into my father's personality, I would say that he is a stranger to no one, a trait both my sister and I were blessed to inherit. He simply loves people. No one is safe from his fun-loving razzing and playful banter. His crowning achievement as king of the capers took place in London, England, at a black-tie affair after I performed in a concert for the late H.R.H. Princess Margaret in 1985. Before arriving at the event, which included an extremely elegant dinner for 20 people, I gave my parents step-by-step instructions on the proper protocol for meeting and greeting royalty. "Do not speak until spoken to. Do not extend a hand to shake unless that hand is first extended to you. And slightly bow upon being introduced." I wasn't at all concerned about my mother, as she inherently knew the appropriate etiquette. My father on the other hand… well let's just say, I know my father all too well.

After introducing my parents to the princess I was relieved that everything had gone off without a hitch. My mother was polite and gracious, and my father was charming and gentlemanly. After a few minutes of small talk, my mother and I—and I assumed my father—followed our escort to our appointed seat. Just as my mother and I were preparing to sit, I heard the sounds of raucous laughter from a voice that sounded all too familiar. My mother and I looked at each other and cringed, wondering, *Oh Lord, what has he done now?* I turned around and there he was, hugging, giggling, and he-he-ing it up with not only the princess, but also her three ladies in waiting as well! My mother gasped! I was mortified! Finally, after what seemed like two weeks, he sauntered over to the table all aglow, basking in the glory of having the undivided attention of *a real* monarch! He had the widest smile I've ever seen on his face.

Just as I was about to reprimand him on breaking the cardinal rules of royal custom, he piped in, "Before you even start, she grabbed and hugged me first!" I doubted his assertion until Princess Margaret began to direct the bulk of her conversation throughout the seven-course meal directly toward my father. Bob Motley had charmed a princess! My mother and I were flabbergasted. On what was to be *my* big night, I was being upstaged, and my mother was trumped by the sister of the queen of England! We have laughed about the evening many times, and it rates as one of our favorite family moments. And needless to say, my mother and I still kid him about that night.

But all kidding aside, Daddy, I thank you for allowing me to take this incredible journey with you and share in the telling of your incredible life story. You have been an inspiration to me and to thousands of other young men, whom you have coached, mentored, counseled, and assisted through the years.

Above all, my sister Bobette and I want you to know how much we honor how you have risen to the occasion of being the primary caretaker for our mother these past several years. We've talked about it often among ourselves but have rarely told you how much we admire and marvel at your commitment to love. Just like everything you have undertaken in life, we have watched you handle this mission, as challenging as it is, with grace and dignity. If we have achieved half the level of devotion, love, and commitment with our respective life partners that you share with Mom, then we too have done okay.

Thank you for being a loving, respectful, and supportive father. I honor you, I respect you, but most of all I love you.

INTRODUCTION
By Bob Motley

I WISH YOU COULD HAVE SEEN all that I have seen. Well, maybe not all, for I have faced some horrendous, life-threatening situations. I have seen death up close, many times too close for comfort. But through it all, I survived and was on hand to witness some incredible moments during my lifetime, particularly those during my umpiring career.

Calling balls and strikes for the Negro Leagues gave me the opportunity to witness first-hand what I consider to be some of the best baseball players in the history of the game. Before the start of every game in which I was the home plate umpire, I was handed a lineup card containing such names as Hank Aaron, Ernie Banks, Willie Mays, Buck O'Neil, Satchel Paige, Willard Brown, and Hilton Smith. I didn't realize it at the time—after all, we were just playing a baseball game—but I was holding history in my hands. Since the league didn't request that umpires send those lineup cards in to the main office or hold onto them for any particular reason, I'd just toss each one in the trash after the game was over. I thought nothing more of it—until today.

It wasn't until the past decade or so that I began talking about my days spent umpiring in the Negro Leagues. Outside of my family and a few close friends, I didn't see the need to share my perspective. As far as most people were concerned, the Negro Leagues were a part of a bygone era that had long since been forgotten. There was no glory in being a member of that league, outside of having survived it. The Negro Leagues weren't widely embraced until recent historians began to uncover hints of the league's greatness that had been ignored for decades. Thanks to the hard work of a few dedicated researchers, filmmakers, and authors, the Negro Leagues are finally beginning to get their just due.

Still, no one has written a book about umpiring in the Negro Leagues. Matter of fact, I'm the only living Negro League umpire—although some days, as I reflect on the life-threatening situations I've encountered in my lifetime, I'm amazed that I'm still among the living.

One story that I like to share—which did *not* happen while I was in the Negro Leagues, but does give a sampling of some of the drama I had to face—occurred as a result of an all-white game that I umpired in the early 1960s. During a time when African-Americans were still fighting for equal footing as citizens in this country, situations could sometimes be tense on the baseball diamond as well. As one of the batters stepped up to the plate, he stared back at me and snarled, "You sure have a lot of nerve umpiring in this league!" I snapped right back. "I sure have! And I got enough nerve to throw you out of this ballgame. Now get outta here!"

An umpire has got to have guts. And for certain, an umpire can count on being no one's friend—at least while on the diamond. An outsider at best, an umpire has to maintain a safe distance from the players he presides over and can never show an iota of favoritism. It makes for a lonely life, one spent on the fringes looking in. A ballplayer enjoys the benefits of being a part of a team—the camaraderie and sense of belonging that comes from bonding with teammates. But an umpire lives in a different world, and hence must adopt a unique disposition. We are stern judges who see the world in black and white. Rules are rules. We are not emotionally invested in a game or swayed by public opinion; we can't be. Had I been better educated and caught a few breaks, I'm sure I could have been a terrific trial lawyer!

Participating in the game as an observer, an overseer, and a mediator, an umpire has the awesome responsibility to be as fair and accurate a judge as humanly possible. There is little reward for those who perform well. Ballplayers celebrate big victories with their teammates; but an umpire doesn't have anything at stake in a particular team's wins or losses. A good umpire gets the same spine-tingling thrill out of making a correct call in a key situation.

As you can see, umpiring is definitely not for everyone; it takes an individual who has a strong constitution and resilience, one that can stand up to irate players, coaches, or fans while maintaining his or her cool. The umpire is often the butt of jokes and the target of outrage when things don't go a team's way. Not everyone can deal with that sort of pressure on a daily basis.

But umpires survive because of a love of the game. And I absolutely loved my 25 years as an umpire for the Negro Leagues, the minor leagues, and beyond. Fortunately, I did hang on to a few items from my Negro League days. Leaving the stadium after a game, I would sometimes have a pocket full of baseballs, which I would usually toss to the kids who were hanging around in the parking lot. But I did keep a couple of those baseballs for myself, and they are now prized possessions. Although the wording has turned faint with age, on the soft spot of one ball you can clearly read the words: "Rawlings—Negro American League—J. B. Martin, President." On another ball I handwrote, "All-Star Game—August 31, 1955—Chicago, Ill.," marking a game I participated in at the time.

Memories are all that any of us have left of the Negro Leagues, so it's important that those of us who participated in those games keep the spirit of the league alive for future generations. As you go on this journey with me in the pages that follow, I hope you enjoy the glimpse into one man's time spent ruling over Monarchs, Giants, and Stars.

1

YOU'RE OUTTA HERE!

Mother, may I slug the umpire
May I slug him right away?
So he cannot be here, Mother
When the clubs begin to play?
Let me climb his frame, dear mother,
While the happy people shout;
I'll not kill him, dearest mother
I will only knock him out.

* From the anonymous poem, "Slug The Umpire" *

IN MY DAY, THE UMPIRE traveled with the team while on the road. On barnstorming trips, the Kansas City Monarchs would take a managing crew with them. So on several occasions, I got to travel with the team as they dotted the Midwest countryside with baseball exhibitions.

For an umpire, traveling with the team can be a troublesome proposition. Not only did I have to call a fair game, I also had to answer to the players and coaches on the bus ride to the next town. Trapped on a bus for hours on end, I had nowhere to run if a player took exception to a call I had made and wanted to make sure I knew he was upset. I had gotten into several brief debates with players while on such bus rides, but never had I felt truly threatened. Most players surprisingly stayed out of my way—until one night when I received a wake-up call I'll never forget.

During a night game in Chattanooga, Tennessee, I made a strike three call on Kansas City Monarchs infielder Hank Bayliss. The opposing pitcher threw a beautiful curve ball by him that nipped the outside corner of the plate. I called him out, and Bayliss turned toward me and began cussing, fussing, and storming around like a child having a temper tantrum. He was furious! I think he was probably madder at himself for not swinging at strike three than he actually was at me, but he decided to take it out on the ol' umpire.

I watched his rant, taking no action until he committed baseball's ultimate no-no: he bumped into me. Today, major and minor league players and coaches are fined big bucks if they touch an umpire, regardless of whether it's on purpose or not. In the Negro Leagues there were no such fines. The only repercussion for an umpire was to exercise his authority and toss the player out of the game—which is precisely what I did. Bayliss was already dead meat when he cursed at me, but after purposely bumping into me, he was definitely a goner.

Bayliss made sure to make a show of it after I threw him out: he held up the game for a good five minutes, arguing still some more and calling me a sack full of "motherfucker"s. Once a player is ejected from a game, he is supposed to go directly into the clubhouse, out of sight of the game and the umpire. But Bayliss was having none of that. Instead, he sat defiantly on the team bench and continued spouting profanities in my direction.

Fed up, I marched over to the bench and told him sternly, "Now I done warned you for the last time. Get off this bench—you're out of the game. I don't wanna see your face." Buck O'Neil, the Monarchs manager, stepped in and tried to coax Bayliss into the clubhouse, but that fool wouldn't budge. Finally, I threatened to clear the entire bench and forfeit the game if Bayliss didn't make a swift exit. He stormed off, slamming bats, gloves, and everything else in his path to the ground as he descended into the clubhouse. To add insult to injury, the Monarchs ended up losing the game.

As I stepped onto the Monarchs' bus after the game, I could have cut the tension with a knife. Every player sat there glaring at me. I would've just as soon walked to the next town rather than take a seat on that bus. But I couldn't back down from the team—doing so would have meant losing respect and sacrificing my authority. So as usual, I ambled to the back of the bus and settled in for a long bus ride.

Thanks to my military background, I had developed an innate sense of my surroundings. It wasn't that I was paranoid, just cautious. And on this particular night, even though the bus ride was quiet, I could sense that something wasn't right. Shortly after I began umpiring, I got a taste for how worked up some players could get when things didn't go their way, so I made a vow to myself to never take for granted what an unhappy player may have in store for retribution. As a rule, I kept my facemask nearby on every bus ride just in case I needed to protect myself against a player or manager who might want to act a fool.

On this night, my strategy came in handy. Bayliss, still seething from my strike three call, waited until the bus had driven into the darkest stretch of the secluded Tennessee highway. When everyone was fast asleep, he made his move. Lucky for me, I was a light sleeper on those bus rides. I woke up immediately when I heard his footsteps stomping toward me. Bayliss was not a large man, under 6 foot and maybe 175 pounds, so I knew I could take him in a fistfight. But he wasn't looking for a fair fight: he was coming right at me with a damn butcher's knife! Once he saw that I was awake, he began shouting, "You goddamn, no good, blind motherfucking Motley—I'm gonna kill your black ass!" As he lunged at me, I instinctively swung at him with my facemask. Thankfully we both missed each other. Buck O'Neil, the ever-mindful skipper, ran all the way down the aisle from the front of the bus and jumped between us in the blink of an eye.

Buck then reamed Bayliss something fierce. "Bayliss, you ignorant bastard! Do you wanna ruin you and your family's life by hurting this umpire, and then have to go to jail over a goddamn baseball game? You touch that umpire again and I'm gonna throw your ass off this bus and you will never—you hear me *never*—play another ballgame in this league again. Now go sit your ass back down and act like you got some damn sense!"

Buck's words reverberated throughout the bus, waking up the team and driving home an important point: don't mess with the ump. I never had any more problems with Bayliss or any other Monarchs player from that day forward.

The events of that night may have caused a weaker man to question his chosen profession. But growing up in the South, and later serving in the Marines during World War II, I had grown accustomed to such narrow escapes.

2
SAFE AT HOME

"To move away from the South required money,
and to accumulate money was not easy."
* Jackie Robinson *

I SHOULD'VE BEEN DEAD a long time ago. If growing up in the harshness of the segregated South with the Ku Klux Klan making frequent drive-bys past my house didn't kill me, then being attacked by crazed ballplayers and rabid fans during my tenure in the Negro Leagues should have done the job. Certainly the bullets that whizzed past my head during my military service in World War II should've done me in. But God has been gracious enough to grant me a long, prosperous, and adventurous life. For that I am grateful.

My life's journey began on March 11, 1923 in Autaugaville, Alabama, a small town located halfway between Selma and Montgomery in the middle of the state. That region of the country is often referred to as "the deep South," "Jim Crow territory," and "the land of Dixie." But I have always affectionately referred to it as "red clay country." Throughout Alabama and a good part of the South, the soil has a beautiful, rich, burgundy hue that makes it look as if it's been soaked by the blood of Civil War soldiers. As kids, we used to eat the clay because our elders told us it was full of vitamins and nutrients. I was sure that munching on it from time to time would help me grow up to be big and strong. Tell me it's just an old wives' tale, but I believe there's some truth to the folklore. Yes I do.

I was the sixth of eight children born to William Motley and Eula Inez Parker Motley. When I was four years old, my daddy died from drinking tainted well water on our property. To this day, I don't know how the water went bad. When I was a child it was never discussed—at least not in front of me. As adults, my siblings and I speculated that someone who was disgruntled with Daddy might have poisoned the well, because water rarely went bad on its own. It is highly possible a member of the Ku Klux Klan was responsible. We also considered that a black person who was jealous of Daddy's desires to expand his farming venture might have done the deed. But it's a question that will never be answered.

I have no memories of my father. As a child, my mind ran wild with thoughts of what Daddy must have been like, and what it would be like to have him around. Today, even when I look at the one weather-beaten picture of this brown-skinned, imposing man that was discovered years after his death, I still have no recollection of him. Seeing a hint of myself in his image riles my curiosity all the more.

Daddy had been a sharecropper, farming cotton and corn for a white family that lived nearby. He had dreams of developing his own farm to supplement his income and care for his ever-growing brood. Daddy's family was poor farming folk, without much formal education to speak of. Considering the times, he was just a typical, poor black man struggling to make a way for himself and his family.

Mama's family, on the other hand, was somewhat well-to-do. The Parkers had plenty of land and were upwardly mobile, or at least as upwardly mobile as black folks could be in red clay country during Jim Crow's reign.

In the absence of my father, my paternal role models were my older brothers—James, William ("Buddy"), Otto, and Felmon. In turn, my sibling responsibility was to help bring up my younger brothers, George and Donnie. However, the sibling who had the biggest impact and influence on me was my big sister, Geraldine. The third oldest, she was more like a second mother than a sister to us kids. Geraldine took up the slack and helped Mama around the house with all the womanly chores. My big sis loved all her brothers, but I like to think I was her favorite, as throughout my childhood and adult life I remained closest to her.

The rock of the family was Mama, a chestnut-colored, statuesque woman whose maternal side of the family was mixed with some Indian blood. Her high cheekbones, silky hair, and easy manner were indicative of her heritage. Mama was a very personable and pleasant lady with a sound sense of herself and a big, generous heart. She was also a God-fearing woman who believed in doing the right thing, and she reared her children to be of like mind. The entire family attended the Macedonia Baptist Church, located right down the road from our house. I doubt Mama ever missed a service—even after us kids were grown up. Attending church was not optional in the Motley household. Each Sunday, we would get dressed up in our only good "Sunday going to meeting" outfits and make the three-block trek down the road, rain or shine.

Mama took care of family, friends, and strangers alike. She would give you the shirt off her back if necessary. If a stranger showed up at our house who was traveling through our tiny community, she would fix a sack of food that would include fried chicken or fish, yams, and biscuits and send the stranger lovingly on his way. In those days people weren't leery of strangers as they are now. It was common practice to assist someone who was looking for a handout. Similarly, if family was visiting from out of town, all eight of us kids—and Mama, too—would give up our beds and sleep on the floor, so that our guests would be comfortable.

After Daddy died, Mama washed and ironed clothes for several white families in order to earn a living. We kids would have to pick up the clothes and bring them back to Mama; after she had done her bit, we'd then deliver the clothing back to the white folks. All that hard work didn't leave Mama much time for nonsense. She was stern with us kids, disciplining us when necessary. Even when I was 16 years old and had gotten "too big for my britches," Mama still had no problem making me cut down a "switch" from the nearby oak tree, which she would then use on my bottom. God forbid I'd bring back a puny twig, because then Mama would go out herself and rip off the biggest limb she could find. Mama made us kids strip down for our beatings: "Take them clothes off! I ain't beating no clothes," she would tell the guilty party before delivering an ass whipping. Man, talk about pain: after Mama was done with my behind, I never thought about messing up again.

Lashings aside, I had a wonderful relationship with Mama, though I wouldn't say we were friends. Parent-child relationships in those days were different than they are today, but the love we shared was deep. I had the utmost respect for her and never talked back; she responded in kind in her usual, nurturing way. To this day I'm still amazed at her ability to raise that many children.

I DON'T KNOW ALL THE INS AND OUTS of the situation, but immediately following Daddy's death, the tainted well was permanently covered up, and our family was whisked off to a new life and home in Anniston, Alabama. Mama's three brothers chipped in and bought us a house at 1109 Union Hill Road in an area everyone called "Buttermilk Road." The house was a small but pleasant two-bedroom, wood-framed home that was built up off the ground on slats. We had a living room, dining room, kitchen (with an old wood-burning stove and an ice box), front porch, outhouse, and plenty of acreage. Mama and Geraldine slept in one bedroom, and all the boys slept in the other, three to a bed. James, my oldest brother, slept in the living room.

For a five-year-old mind like mine, our new life in Anniston seemed like we had moved to the big city. Anniston was about 150 miles northeast of Autaugaville, and around 65 miles east of Birmingham, Alabama. Even though our new home was in the rural, segregated area of town, the "white-only" downtown was less than three miles away. There, one could find a rail station, nice storefronts, shops, offices, hotels, bars, and other establishments. Autaugaville had nothing like that.

Anniston was my first experience living in a decent-sized community with plenty of black folks who looked out for each other. We had to, because the Ku Klux Klan was always around. The Klan provided plenty of drama for my family. My Uncle Buddy, one mean son-of-a-bitch, lived in a modest shotgun shack in the woods about a mile from our house. His wife had left him after one too many beatings, so my uncle lived alone, a recluse. Well, he wasn't entirely on his own. Besides the acres of land he claimed as his and that tiny tin shack he called his home, he kept company with a donkey and a pack of about 40 dogs. He loved those dogs, but whenever one failed to obey him he'd shoot the poor animal without thinking twice.

Four or five times a week, Uncle Buddy would come to our house early in the morning for breakfast. We'd see him coming over

9

the hill riding on his donkey with a pack of yappy dogs obediently following him. It was a hilarious, yet bizarre, sight to see. Those dogs followed him everywhere. When he arrived, he'd park the donkey out front and come barreling into the house. "How y'all kids doing?" he'd ask. Before we could answer he'd holler at the top of his lungs, "Inez, where's my food?" Without saying a word, Mama would get in the kitchen and whip up some biscuits and gravy or bacon, eggs, and grits. He'd slop down his breakfast like it was his first and last meal, then snarl, "Inez, that food wasn't shit!" It wouldn't phase Mama one bit. She'd sweetly reply, "You're welcome, Buddy. See you tomorrow?" He never answered. Out the door he'd be, back on that ol' broken-down donkey, with his mob of wild dogs in tow and his gun on the side of his hip.

Word got out that the Ku Klux Klan was out to get Uncle Buddy. I have no idea why, but his name had made the dreaded hit list. Maybe the white folks just wanted those acres of land he had taken for himself. We all were fearful that Uncle Buddy's days were numbered, because usually when the Klan was coming to get you, your black ass was done for. However, when the Klan stepped foot on his property, Uncle Buddy turned all those dogs loose and the Klan took off running, as he said, "like a bunch of sissies from a whore in a cocktail dress." Uncle Buddy gloated as he recapped the story for us, proud of his victory. We were in awe, because it was unheard of for a black man to stand up to the Klan. But to my knowledge, the Klan never bothered Uncle Buddy again.

The Klan always did its dirty work at night. Since Union Hill Road, which led past our house, was the only through street in the black section of town, the Klan would often drive right past us on its way to a lynching or cross-burning ceremony. We could always hear them coming from three or four blocks away, as they would honk their horns like they were heading to a parade. Several cars would go speeding by with the passengers decked out in their infamous white-hooded robes, sounding like a bunch of crazed banshees. Some of the more animated ones rode on the hoods and trunks, or hung out of the windows shouting as they sped by. It was a frantic, idiotic revelry to witness. I never could see their faces so I had no idea who they were. Mama would always say, "It's better we don't know." If a black man tried to snoop into their world, then he'd be missing before the sun came up.

Upon hearing even the faintest sound of a car horn, Mama would shout with a quiver of panic in her voice, "Y'all kids hurry up and turn off them lights and lay down on the floor. Here they come!" With the house pitch black we'd crawl up to the window and peek out without uttering a word, fearful that the slightest sound or movement might catch their attention. Even my older brother, Otto, who was no stranger to trouble, knew enough to keep his head down and his mouth shut when the Klan was near. I could hear my heart pound with terror as I lay there. As often as these drive-bys occurred, it never became commonplace—the fear was *always* intense and chilling.

On those nights it would be hard to fall asleep; the fear wouldn't subside until we'd hear the Klan return two or three hours later, after they had finished their business. If their drive back was quiet, then we breathed a sigh of relief, figuring that they were unsuccessful in finding a victim. But if their return had the celebratory refrain of rifles shooting in the air and car horns blaring, then we knew some poor black soul had been lynched just over the hill.

Thankfully, I never had any run-ins with the Klan. That was my greatest fear. Mama had always stressed to us kids to be careful and respectful of all white folks. She didn't want to have to bury any of her children for making the simple mistake of speaking out of line. Lord knows she might have buried her husband because of it.

Some of those horrific memories of life in the South are thoughts that I would like to be able to forget. But those images and sounds have stayed with me throughout the years. As I reflect today, I don't think the red dirt of the South is from the blood of Civil War soldiers at all, but rather from the thousands of black souls who still cry out for justice. Maybe that's why black folks told me that the ground was full of vitamins and nutrients, and why I did grow up to be so big and strong.

JOHN WILSON LIVED right across the road from us. When I was eight years old, he was in his 60s or early 70s, an old man as far as I was concerned. The combination of his age, his soft-spoken demeanor, and the fact that he was slow on his feet made him seem grandfatherly. Everyone in my family liked Mr. Wilson because of his gentle spirit, his understated elegance, and the fact that he had money. I don't know how he had initially acquired his money, but he had done all right for himself. His wealth made him stand out amongst the blacks and whites: He was the only black man at the time to own a business on Noble Street, the main street of downtown Anniston. At his furniture store, he peddled antique chairs, sofas, ottomans, tables, lamps, and a variety of other household items. He was also the only person in our neighborhood who owned a car. From the time I knew him as a child until he died in his 90s, Mr. Wilson always bought himself a brand-new car every two years or so. That always amazed us kids.

I got to know Mr. Wilson better because his grandson, Edward, was my first friend outside my family. Edward Wilson was about my age, and we became fast friends. Like his grandpa, Edward was chocolate dark with kinky hair and distinct facial features. Whereas all of us Motley children were of different hues, which I attribute to our Indian blood (and rumored white blood from slavery days), the Wilsons were definitely direct African descendants.

Edward and his grandpa lived by themselves in a house that overflowed with furniture and items from Mr. Wilson's store, forcing visitors to step around and over mounds of antiques just to maneuver through the house. Once every year or so, Edward's parents would make the journey from Gaston, Alabama, and visit for a few days. Sometimes Edward would go back with them for a short visit, but he always returned to be with his grandpa. While Edward was away, Mr. Wilson would turn grumpy and lose his spirit; but when Edward returned, Mr. Wilson would light up like a firecracker. They had a father/son-type bond that was completely foreign to me, and I often envied it.

As we all were, Mama was also attentive to Mr. Wilson. She often took him meals and checked in on him from time to time to make sure he was doing okay. We didn't realize it at the time, but Mama had another purpose for visiting Mr. Wilson. He must not have been as frail nor as old as my young mind assumed, because soon our household expanded from eight children to ten. Apparently during Mama's visits she and Mr. Wilson were sharing a little more than just neighborly chitchat. By the time I was ten, I had two new stepsisters, Annie Inez and Queen Esther.

We were all shocked to say the least. But, as it was when Daddy died, no one spoke of it. I knew that my new sisters had taken his surname, but other than that, I stayed out of it. In those days, children didn't pry into grown folks' business. I just figured since Ann and Queen Esther were now my sisters, it meant that my best friend Edward was also my new brother, if only in spirit, and that was fine with me.

LIKE ALL THE CHILDREN in our neighborhood, I attended the Macedonia School, a one-room schoolhouse located in our church.

We had one teacher, Ms. Rowe, who taught all the grades from kindergarten to eighth. Looking back, it's a wonder we learned anything at all with 60 or so kids in one room with one teacher. I don't know how Ms. Rowe was able to maintain our focus on the curriculum and keep all of us under control, but she did. I tip my hat to her for her having the wherewithal to master that feat.

Ms. Rowe loved all of her students, and we loved her, too. She was especially fond of all the Motley children, and often doted on us more than the other kids. Mama had a profound respect for Ms. Rowe because she was enamored by the fact that a black woman could be so educated. In the late 1920s in the Deep South, well-educated Negroes were a rare breed.

School was challenging for me. Lucky for me, Ms. Rowe was patient, often spending extra time with me, as she did when teaching me to write in cursive. In those days, we couldn't choose to only concentrate on schoolwork like kids can do nowadays. In my family, we all had work to do around the house before *and* after school. Besides toting laundry for Mama, my other chores at one point or another included cleaning the house, taking care of the livestock, cleaning the chicken coop, and various other tasks. Early on I developed a work ethic that would become second nature to me in the years to come. But it didn't leave a lot of time for schoolwork.

Our education was basic: We were taught the three Rs— reading, writing, and arithmetic. We didn't learn anything about science, history, or any other subject. And the truth is, we probably wouldn't have been that interested, anyway. Ms. Rowe gave us what she thought would be the most useful tools for our lives. Considering the times, poor black kids weren't supposed to amount to anything, so Ms. Rowe focused on skills that would help us survive. Whatever we lacked in education was made up for with something that black southerners call "mother wit," an inner sense of strength that comes from our familial and cultural experience. In other words, common sense.

One of my first jobs away from home was cleaning up the schoolhouse after school. Edward and I would sweep, clean, and mop the floors on a daily basis. I was earning some money, but I never saw a dime of it. As was common in my family, the money went directly to Mama.

Edward and I didn't have a lot of free time, but whenever we could escape the daily routines of our chores, we would head off into the woods to play. We didn't have any of the luxuries that kids enjoy these days—Hot Wheels or video games—so we made good use of our imaginations and invented our own games. We'd swing from trees, run races through the woods, and throw rocks. As elementary as it sounds, throwing rocks was our favorite pastime. Our aim got so good that I'm sure the birds, squirrels, rabbits, and raccoons that inhabited the wooded area dreaded hearing our footsteps as we'd come stomping into their territory.

Thanks to my four older brothers, I learned that there was more to playing outdoors than throwing rocks at the wildlife. My brother Felmon was the most athletic of all my brothers. To this day, I still think he could have played pro football, as he was a hell of a defensive tackle in high school. Had he pursued it, he could have been the first black man to make it in professional sports. Instead, that honor would eventually go to another Motley, my distant cousin Marion Motley, who integrated the NFL in 1946.

One fateful day, Felmon brought home a small, round, white object with a strange red stitching. He told me it was a baseball, and that the game was all the rage at his new high school. Daily, Edward and I began playing barehanded catch with that ball instead of throwing rocks. We didn't have any knowledge of the game of baseball, so we went back to our old game; the creatures in the woods now had a larger object to dodge. But over the next few months, I received an introduction to my first and longest-lasting love. Felmon taught Edward, my other brothers, and me the basics of baseball. He was a great teacher and coach and enjoyed showing off his athletic prowess to our amazement. The more I learned, the more I fell in love with this fascinating new sport.

When Edward and I had eventually worn out or lost a baseball, we'd make our own. A rock wrapped in a rag and tied with a string made a great substitute. These invented "balls" were lopsided, wobbly, and hard as hell, but it didn't matter to us as long as we could play our new game. Our bats were tree limbs we'd tear down, or, if we were lucky enough, someone would score the handle to a broom, ax, or shovel. There was plenty of open land around, so finding a place to play was no problem. Soon our band of players increased to most of the boys from school. Since I was an expert rock thrower, I naturally gravitated toward pitching. I became confident that one day I was going to develop into one of the best pitchers the game of baseball had ever seen.

I could have played baseball all day and all night. I would daydream throughout school or church service, imagining myself throwing the ball so hard that I would burn a hole through the trunk of those oak trees at home. Sundays were our big baseball day, and church couldn't finish up soon enough. Once I finished my usual prayers for my family, I'd pray for Pastor Hughley to hurry up and finish his sermon so we could get out of there and get a game going. The second church was over, we'd bolt out the door and head up to the top of Buttermilk Road and play until we were ready to pass out or darkness fell—whichever came first.

Mama hated baseball. She wanted us to work. After all, we were poor, and "poor folks didn't have time for no leisure activities," Mama often reminded us. "Robert, that ball and you ain't gonna amount to a hill of beans. Learn your studies and keep yourself a job," she demanded. But it was too late: I was hooked.

Baseball was beginning to get such a grip on me that I prayed Mama would come to understand and appreciate my growing passion. Sadly, she never did.

EVERY SATURDAY MY SISTER GERALDINE went to town to run errands for Mama, and I was often allowed to tag along. I loved those outings. For one, it got me out of the drudgery of my daily chores. But I also knew that Mama had given Geraldine a little extra money to spend as she wanted. On the way back home, we'd stop at a store and buy cheese, crackers, and baloney. We'd eat our snack, laugh, sing, and skip along the railroad tracks all the way back home.

On one of our trips to town, I spotted a little mom and pop grocery store and thought to myself, *I sure would like to work at that store.* The store was tiny, but it was a full-fledged market that sold all types of canned goods, breads, meal, sugar, candy, cookies, and live chickens. The next weekend, I wrote a note, forged Mama's signature, and presented it to the storeowner, a white man named Locker Burns. In my best possible penmanship that I had learned from Ms. Rowe I carefully wrote, "Dear Mister, we are hungry and need money. Will you please hire my son? Sincerely, Inez Motley." Mr. Burns hired me on the spot. I was only ten years old but had finagled my first real job.

Every morning before school I would be at the store bright and early at 6:30 a.m., ready for my duties as janitor and stock boy. I always made sure I arrived before Mr. Burns, a gray-haired, pudgy man with rosy red cheeks—a countrified Santa Claus in overalls and a flannel shirt. He moved like molasses, and talked like it too, with a long, thought-out, southern drawl. Mr. Burns appreciated my enthusiasm and paid me what I considered a handsome salary at that time, a whopping four dollars a week. Every cent I earned, as always, I took home and gave to Mama, who was initially surprised by my resourcefulness but delighted by the extra income.

The store always had a steady flow of regulars, and from what I could tell, Mr. Burns was making money hand over fist. Two years into the job I showed up at my usual hour, waited and waited, but no Mr. Burns. For three days I went back until finally his wife arrived and informed me that Mr. Burns had died of a sudden heart attack. I was deeply saddened because he had become more than just my boss, he had become the first white person I had ever considered to be a friend.

Mr. Burns and I had discovered we shared a common love of baseball. He gave me my first baseball glove, a hand-me-down from one of his sons that I wore out in no time flat. But even better than the glove was all the history of the game he shared with me. I was a novice, having never even seen a real game, but Mr. Burns had seen it all. He educated me on the game, and my young mind struggled to absorb it all. He loved talking about rules and strategy, then quizzed me to see how much I had retained. He would regale me with stories that were so vivid that I could almost picture the players and smell the outfield grass. For the first time, I heard about the greats: Babe Ruth, Rogers Hornsby, Ty Cobb, Casey Stengel, Walter Johnson, Grover Cleveland Alexander, Lefty Grove, and Lou Gehrig. He was also the first person to tell me about a league that existed for "you people" that he said had some good players, too.

Mr. Burns also introduced me to the role of the umpire. I was intrigued because he kept referring to the umpire as the "silent man of the diamond, but the one who controls the game." Mr. Burns laughed as I asked, "But what position does he play?" and, "When does he get to bat?" Finally, after some more clarification, I got it.

After Mr. Burns died, his wife informed me that she was closing the store because she knew nothing about the business.

Knowing the bond that had developed between her husband and me, she told me not to fret about losing my job; she had arranged a new job for me as a bellboy at the Jefferson Davis Hotel. I was to start the next day.

The Burns' lived at the hotel, which was located in the heart of downtown Anniston. The stately, three-story brick structure stood at the corner of 13th and Noble Street. It was a 160-room, white-only establishment that to my 12-year-old eyes looked like a skyscraper. The intimidation didn't last long, however, as I soon became accustomed to my new job. I worked hard, and within two years I had become the hotel's first-ever black doorman.

The Jefferson Davis was a hub for both transient and permanent residents. All the elite people stayed there: celebrities, ballplayers, politicians, you name it. If they were white and had money, when they came to Anniston, they stayed at the Jefferson Davis Hotel—named after the honorable (or not so honorable, depending on how you look at history) Jefferson Davis, the only president of the Confederate States of America. Back then, there were a lot of buildings and monuments dedicated in Davis' name in the South. One of our residents, a crotchety old lady named Mrs. Faulk, even had a wiry, little black dog she called "Jeffie Davis." I found the irony of naming a black dog after one of the country's staunchest segregationists to be idiotic, but quite humorous. I must admit I preferred hearing Mrs. Faulk summon "Jeffie," as opposed to hearing another old white woman (who also lived at the hotel) summon her black dog, "Nigger." Many times while walking through the lobby I'd hear her say, "Come here, Nigger." After a few weeks, I finally got over the instinct to respond "Yes, ma'am" upon hearing her command.

The older I got the more independent I became. Instead of giving all of my earnings from my new job to Mama, I began keeping a cut for myself. After a year of working at the hotel, I had saved up enough money to buy myself a bicycle, which I rode to and from work and school. My younger brothers and buddies always wanted to borrow it or get a ride somewhere. Possessing a burgeoning entrepreneurial spirit, I decided that charging a nickel a ride would be a smart move. That extra money came in handy when I wanted to buy goodies that I had been without for so long.

Money wasn't the only perk of working at the hotel. I also met my first professional athletes, a team of minor league baseball players, at the hotel. Teams from the Southeastern League that Mr. Burns had told me about—which included the Atlanta Crackers, Birmingham Barons, Greensboro Bats, Memphis Chicks, Nashville Sounds, and Montgomery Wings—were frequent guests at the hotel when they played games nearby or were traveling between cities. Their team bus would pull up in front of the hotel, and the players would bound off, sometimes in their uniforms, other times in street clothes. As far as I was concerned, these guys were major leaguers. They sure handled themselves that way. They were confident, fit, and dignified. I thought that must be how all professional athletes carried themselves. I was so impressed that I began to mimic their actions, because I was sure that somehow, someday I too would be a professional ballplayer.

The ballplayers were always gentlemen. I didn't have many dealings with them after checking them into their rooms, because they pretty much stuck to themselves. But they were always personable, and they tipped well, too. They were nothing like the soldiers who stayed at the Jefferson Davis Hotel. A few miles from the hotel on the east end of Anniston was the Fort McClellan Army Base. Some people considered it the pride of Anniston. There wasn't much industry in the city to speak of, so townspeople had to find pride in something. The first and 15th of every month was payday for the soldiers, and many of them would check into the Jefferson Davis looking for booze and girls. Soon, the entrepreneur in me got a taste of the big time.

My fellow bellman, George Cannon, was probably in his 50s at the time, and, judging from his outrageous stories, had been around the block a few times. George was a short, brown-skinned man with severely bowed legs. He was boisterous to the point of being obnoxious, but he always kept me laughing, and he was a hard worker. George was not a well-educated man, but he made up for that with street smarts. He turned the job of bell hopping into an art, and took me under his wing, teaching me the ins and outs of how to make extra money from our craft.

George made a second paycheck off the soldiers. A few days before the soldiers' arrival at the hotel, George and I would gather up four or five empty suitcases and board the Southern Pacific railroad line to Birmingham, about an hour away by train. So that we weren't questioned when we boarded, George passed me off as his son. When we arrived in Birmingham we would head straight to a liquor store in the black section of town that George was familiar with, and then stock up with half pints of booze. Our suitcases would be filled with every bottle of liquor on the shelf: bourbon, scotch, whiskey, gin, rum, and a variety of brands including Bacardi, Dewar's, Jameson, and Johnny Walker. You name it, we had it.

Back at the hotel, we would stash the goods in the coal bins in the basement, since we were the only employees who had access to that area. When the soldiers would arrive with their pockets full of money, we were more than happy to take it from them in exchange for booze. Two dollars would buy a guy whatever liquor he fancied. George and I would split the profits.

We weren't the only ones profiting from the men in uniform. The ladies of the night knew the soldiers' schedule as well. Once I got used to the game, I could spot one of "the girls," as George and I called them, as she came traipsing through the lobby hoping to find herself "a date." These women were not floozies or trashy-looking street prostitutes; no, they were well-groomed, attractive ladies. If I didn't know they were there for business, I would have assumed they were just average hotel guests.

Very seldom would "the girls" show up alone. They'd either be with a man (whom I assumed was their pimp) or another woman. Being the bellhop, it was my job to escort every guest to his or her room with bags in tow. When it came to "the girls," once the elevator doors closed the ladies would let me know they were "here for business." My job then was to deliver to them the soldiers who were looking for a good time, which was most of them. I prided myself on pairing up a particular solider with a girl I thought he might like. It was probably my way of acting out my own fantasies, since I was a teenager with raging hormones.

I always treated the ladies with respect, and in return they were always respectful to me as well. Long before I knew the tricks of the trade, George had already established a rapport with the girls, so it was understood that once a "trick" was delivered, we'd get a cut of the proceeds. I'd usually end up getting about two or three dollars per delivery. And sometimes, if the soldier had really enjoyed himself, he'd toss me a couple extra bucks as a "thank you" tip as well. Some nights, between the liquor and the girls, I'd end up with well over a hundred dollars. I still took money home to Mama to help out with the family, but I also kept more of a fair share for myself. Had Mama known how tainted that money was, she wouldn't have needed the Klan to carry out her dirty work—she would've hung me up from a tree herself.

It wasn't long before I was dealing left and right. I was a born negotiator. In addition to hustling booze and broads, I made a sweet deal for my own transportation. I had gotten friendly with all the white taxi drivers in town because of the business I supplied them from the hotel. The drivers took care of me as well, arranging to have me picked up in the mornings at 5 a.m. from my house, taken to work, then to school, then back to work, and finally home again at the end of the day. Colored people were forbidden to ride in white taxis in Jim Crow's South. But here I was, being chauffeured about town like a black prince in his personal chariot. It's a wonder the Klan didn't have me tarred and feathered, but the drivers treated me like an equal. Obviously, the color of my skin didn't matter to them as long as I was bringing them business.

When I turned 16 I was earning enough money from bell hopping, booze, and broads that I was able to buy my first car, a black 1937 Ford coupe with a 65-horsepower engine. Although it was a used car, that coupe was my new baby. I was the first of all my peers to have my own car. I was moving up in the world. For the first time in my life, I was also able to buy myself some decent clothes, including a brand-new suit, shirts, slacks, ties, and a couple of fedoras. I was stylin' beyond belief.

One day I decided to show off my new ride and take my younger brothers on a day trip to Opelika, Alabama, about a hundred miles south of Anniston. George and Donnie had never been outside of Anniston, and I wanted to give them a treat. Even though I was on the verge of manhood, Mama still demanded that I make it home before dark. When the three of us came strolling in the house long after the appointed curfew, Mama was sitting in the front room waiting on us. With switches already in hand and a pail of scalding hot water sitting beside her to ensure that we wouldn't run away, she whipped us something good that night! After that, I can guarantee you I was always home long before the sun went down.

By the time I was 16, all of my older brothers had escaped the South and had started new lives for themselves elsewhere. My brother William was living in Dayton, Ohio, and had written to me several times, encouraging me to join him there. From his descriptions, Ohio sounded like paradise to me, and I longed to go. Mama thought it was a good idea too, even though I hadn't finished high school yet. She insisted it would be safer to hop the train instead of driving such a long distance. So on a chilly October day in 1939, I headed down to the railroad station with a box full of fried chicken, biscuits, yams, and other goodies that Mama had prepared for me; four pockets and a knapsack full of money; some clothes; and my treasured baseball glove in hand. I waited for the northbound Southern Pacific, and when the coast was clear, I hopped aboard a freight car and joined the rest of the hobos who, like me, were venturing northward to a new life. A dozen black souls of all ages were crammed together on our way to a promised land of jobs, independence, and a better life for a colored man in America.

As the train chugged forward, I could feel the weight of Southern oppression being lifted off my shoulders. On that long ride north, I thought about the opportunity that lay ahead: to prove myself worthy of whatever life had in store for this southern country boy.

3
FINDING THE RIGHT UNIFORM

"Freedom is a hard-bought thing and millions are in chains,
but they strain toward the new day drawing near."
* Paul Robeson *

IT SEEMED LIKE IT TOOK THAT TRAIN five years to get from Anniston, Alabama, to Dayton, Ohio, but in reality it was only a couple of days. The ride gave me time to reflect on what I wanted from life. Mama's mantra, "Self-preservation is the first law of nature," had been drilled into my head from as far back as I could remember. This was my first time away from home, my first chance to explore a world outside of Anniston, my first chance to spend quality time with myself. This was indeed my first chance at life. I decided to take full advantage of the situation: I was going to make it on my own. Hopping off the train, a feeling of euphoria, of being free of the South, overwhelmed me. For the first time, my eyes were wide open to a world of hope and opportunity.

Like many northern cities, Dayton was a hub for African-Americans who had left the South in search of a better life. The newcomers like me always stuck out like a sore thumb amongst the blacks whose families had lived in the area for generations. Our manner of dress and talk was a dead giveaway, but I soon learned to adapt quickly to a more citified, cultured way of living.

Dayton was a clean city. The houses, even in the inner city, looked like mansions compared to the shotgun shacks of Anniston. In the black neighborhoods there were blocks and blocks of manicured lawns, with children riding bicycles, girls jumping rope and skipping hopscotch, and boys playing impromptu games of baseball in the middle of the streets. It all seemed idyllic—all these black families living a life that was foreign to me.

Although Dayton was also segregated, the black community was prideful and full of life. Fifth Street, the center of black Dayton life, hummed to the pulse of progressive people of color. Never in my life had I seen so many well-dressed, refined, and educated black people. I was inspired and energized. Intoxicated by my newly discovered sense of self, I chose not to get in touch with my brother right away. Embracing my newly discovered spirit of independence, I decided to take a few days to get the lay of the land, renting a room in a boarding house for $1.50 a day.

The next day I landed a job as a janitor at Patterson Field, a logistics and defense plant that historically played a key role in supporting the Air Corps operations throughout the nation. Toward the end of World War II, Patterson merged with Wright Field and was renamed Wright-Patterson Air Force Base, one of the largest airport installations in the world. I worked at Patterson only briefly, because I soon tired of having to thumb a ride to and from a job that lay about 30 miles outside of town.

Keeping my ear to the ground and eavesdropping on sidewalk conversations, I learned that the Inland Manufacturing Company was hiring. With the strong economic boom that the country was experiencing in the late 1930s and early 1940s, factories and other outlets were popping up all over, making it easy to find work. Established to produce steering wheels for its parent company, General Motors, Inland was also contracted to manufacture the M1 Carbine rifle as the war loomed. My job of reaming out the bullet chambers on rifles was tedious, but it didn't matter as long as I was getting a paycheck. Little did I know that one day soon I would carry one of those weapons into battle.

After I found a place to live and a job I liked, I decided to contact my brother William. William was elated to hear from me, but chided me for not getting in touch with him sooner. Unbeknownst to me, he had done everything but put out an APB in the hopes of locating me. Mama had been worried sick about me since no one had heard from me since I left Alabama. When William arrived at my boarding house he gave me a big brother bear hug that felt like the entire city of Dayton embracing me. At that moment I knew I'd never return to live in the South.

William drove me to meet the patriarch of our family clan, Samuel Parker, my mother's oldest brother. Uncle Samuel had left Alabama years before, and I barely recalled meeting him as a child. Upon entering his home he warmly greeted me with both a handshake and a hug, stating, "Boy, if you ain't the spitting image of your mama." (William later told me that he had been told the same thing.) Uncle Samuel opened his home to me as if I were his own son. "You Inez's boy," he said to me, "which means you *my* boy."

Uncle Samuel invited me to move into his home, but I resisted at first, still determined to go it on my own. But my uncle, using his infinite charm and impressing upon me the importance of family helping family, insisted. And so I took up residence with him and his family at 918 Reist Avenue.

I'm so glad I made that decision. For my early adult years while living in Dayton and beyond, Uncle Samuel became the father figure that I had missed growing up. He was dignified, cultured, always upbeat, and the quintessential gentleman. For me, he redefined the word *class*. He always dressed the role of the dapper gentleman with fashionable suits, ties, and hats. And although he had grown up in the heart of Alabama, he had lost the typical southern drawl that I was accustomed to back home. He was charismatic and witty and a stranger to no one. Friends with blacks as well as whites, his alliances with Dayton's white mayor and other local political figures impressed the heck out of this young, unworldly country boy. Yet despite his upward associations, he was always approachable and humble, a man who seldom spoke of his social standing. But everywhere I went I was known as "Sam Parker's nephew," so I knew that I'd better be on my very best behavior, lest I tarnish his good name and reputation.

Uncle Samuel was a light brown-skinned man with thick wire-rimmed glasses framing his handsome, high-cheekboned face. A fit 6-foot-1, he exuded pride and confidence. He counseled with a fatherly tone, choosing wise words that I took to heart and eventually passed down to my own children. One piece of advice in particular took years to understand, but after some unfortunate disappointments I truly came to grasp its simple profoundness: *"Good or bad, when people show you who they are, believe them."*

Uncle Samuel became my hero. If I could have been nothing else in this world, I wanted to be like him. Here was a proud black man who had made a life for himself. His three-bedroom house was spacious, well furnished, and immaculate. Aunt Lillian took obvious pride in making sure the home was a respite for her family from the outside world. Uncle Samuel's sons, Sam Jr. and Burt, were a bit younger than me and were progressive, educated, young black men who spoke in a dignified manner with even less of a southern drawl than their father. Like their dad, they were always spiffily dressed with an endless wardrobe of sharp slacks and shirts. Also like their father, they were always gentlemen. In time, I would emulate the manners and morals of the entire Parker family. I was quite proud to be a part of the clan.

I accepted sharing a room with my cousin Burt because I had my own bed with decent sheets, a pillow, and a warm, hand-woven wool blanket. Those were small details, but much as my brother had promised in his letters, they all added up to a life of paradise! As I unpacked my meager belongings, Burt was shocked to see that I had a baseball glove.

"You play?" he questioned.

"Sure," I replied without a bit of hesitation.

"I play the outfield," he told me. "What about you?"

"I play all positions," I quipped.

"Wow, you must be good!" he said with youthful enthusiasm.

After a moment we agreed to play catch when we could find a window of time, and proceeded to talk about baseball for the rest of the night. I was still pretty limited in my knowledge of the game and had no real hands-on experience to relate to, although I acted as if I did. I recalled my conversations with Locker Burns and the league he mentioned that was for my people. I asked Burt if he had ever seen any all-black teams play. He chuckled, saying that was all he had seen. In those days, everything was segregated, even in the North, even in America's great pastime. Burt promised that when baseball season arrived he'd take me to see some games. Night after night I lay in bed, barely able to wait for the arrival of spring.

ALTHOUGH I WAS WORKING during the day at Inland and helping William clean office buildings at night, I made sure to take Burt up on his promise to take me to see some ball games. So on a Sunday afternoon in the spring of 1940 we made our way over to Ducks Ballpark on West Third Street to see a game between two local all-black amateur teams, the names of which I have long forgotten.

Walking into that stadium was like walking into heaven. The playing field had brown patches of dead grass mixed with the green. The benches we sat on were rickety and splintered. The stands were hardly full. But none of that mattered: We were at a baseball game! Although I had no idea who any of the players were, I could hear myself cheering the loudest. I was excited for the players, but mostly I was just excited for myself.

Looking back, the level of play of those Dayton teams didn't compare to the future Hall of Famers I would umpire for in the Negro Leagues; but it was a great introduction to black baseball in a city that had a heritage dating back to the 1920s. Earlier in the century, Ducks Ballpark had been home to the all-black Dayton Marcos baseball team. From what I heard from the old-timers who hung out at the park, the Marcos had been the pride of Dayton. Although the franchise was short lived, it had been one of the first professional teams to take root in the city. The Marcos were a charter member in the first Negro National League that was formed in 1920 by legendary black baseball entrepreneur Andrew "Rube" Foster.

Burt and I went back to Ducks Ballpark as often as we could throughout the summer of 1940. I even ventured over to the stadium a couple of times on my own just to see a game or watch the local teams practice. Sometimes I'd spend the 10 cents and buy a ticket; other times I'd peer through the knotholes in the wooden fence outside the stadium.

Black baseball had become a part of my life, and I was about to get a proper introduction to the Negro Leagues. One evening Burt came bounding into our room with a level of excitement I had rarely seen from him. "The Toledo Crawfords are coming to town!" He was almost yelling he was so excited. I didn't want to appear too naïve, but I thought to myself, *The who?* After calming down he explained that the Toledo Crawfords and St. Louis Stars, two teams from the official Negro Leagues, would be making a barnstorming stop in Dayton to play against one another. This was an annual event in Dayton, when at least one of the official Negro League teams came through on an exhibition tour. It was such a huge event that even Uncle Samuel, who never talked about sports, was all keyed up about it. As he put it, he only got excited about baseball when "the real teams came to town."

I didn't know it then, but barnstorming was commonplace in black baseball. Before, during, and after the season teams would travel throughout the country and play in exhibition games to enhance their incomes. To the towns that hosted their games, it was considered an honor. Everywhere I went for the next few weeks, I overheard people talking about the upcoming Negro League game. The town was abuzz with excitement! Placards advertising the game were hung in store windows and were tacked on light poles all throughout the black community. I could tell this was going to be something really special, and indeed it was.

Game day was a Sunday afternoon, and it seemed like the whole black community just stopped in its tracks to attend the game. Churches let out early, and the few establishments that were usually open on Sundays were closed for business as all of black Dayton headed over to Ducks Ballpark. I had never seen so many black folks filing in to one place in my life. Everybody was decked out in their finest attire: The men had on stylish suits and fedoras, and the ladies were dressed to kill in skirts and dresses in every spring-like color one could imagine. Aunt Lillian had prepared a picnic basket full of food for the entire family.

Unlike all the previous times I had been to the stadium, Ducks was bursting at the seams. It was standing room only, and people were everywhere: in the aisles, on top of the dugouts, even sitting on top of one another. The entire stadium looked like a chocolate rainbow, full of brown and black hues. It was a beautiful sight to behold. This experience was life-changing for me. I was experiencing the true love and spirit of baseball. I wanted to *be* on that diamond and hear people cheering for *me*. I decided on that day that one way or another, baseball was going to be my life.

As the two teams prepared to square off, the crowd's enthusiasm grew to a frenzy. Taking in the sights and sounds, I noticed that the stands were dotted with a few white spectators who appeared to be just as enthused as the black folks. I found this to be wondrously curious. Just then, I spotted a couple white umpires on the field of play as well. I leaned over to Uncle Samuel and asked him why those white men were umpiring a black game. Before he could answer, an old man sitting in front of us piped in, "They're there to make sure them spooks out there don't get out of line." Everyone around us got a good laugh out of his quip.

It was actually quite common for white umpires to be used in the Negro Leagues—especially in the early days. Due to the lack of qualified or interested blacks, white umpires had been a staple in the all-black game for many years. Many of the black umpires who were used were often former players who had retired from playing, as I learned when I began umpiring in the leagues. By the time I started umpiring in the Negro Leagues in the late 1940s, the leagues had become more sophisticated, and black umpires were more common. However, in some smaller communities like Dayton there were only a handful of black umpires who were experienced at handling the task, so whites were still being used in those instances.

As the pitcher hurled his first pitch to start the game, I was immediately struck by the superior caliber of play compared to the amateur teams I had been watching at Ducks. There *was* no comparison—*this* was the big leagues for blacks. *These* were the guys Locker Burns spoke about with such high regard. I marveled not only at the skill of the players, but their intensity as well. Batters stretched singles into doubles and doubles into triples with lightning speed. Pitchers zipped balls with such speed across the plate that it was hard to follow the pitch. Runners were sliding and diving into bases with such force, they would actually knock the fielder down.

Unbeknownst to me then, both teams I was watching were stocked with some formidable talent. I recall the fans chanting, "Charlie, Charlie, Charlie" for a stocky yellow slugger who years later I recognized as Oscar Charleston. Now a Hall of Famer, Charleston was player/manager for the Crawfords and one of the most powerful hitters in Negro League history. In this particular game he crushed a towering triple that smacked off the centerfield wall, much to everyone's delight. Jimmy "Crutch" Crutchfield and Sam Bankhead, both outfielders for the Crawfords, were also fan favorites, as was Stars infielder Bobby Robinson.

Secretly thinking that I would someday be a great pitcher myself, I paid special attention to each team's hurler. The standout of the day was the Crawfords' rookie pitcher, and future major leaguer, Clifford "Connie" Johnson. The lanky Johnson mowed down batter after batter with perfect tosses that zoomed by the hitter on the way to the catcher's mitt. He was a whiz on the mound. Little did I know sitting in the stands that day that one day I would be behind the plate calling balls and strikes for this fantastic pitcher.

After the game everyone lingered in the stadium while talking about the game and enjoying the fellowship. It was obvious the fans did not want the celebration to end. And neither did I. In the weeks following the game, I was on a baseball high. All I wanted to do was talk baseball, baseball, baseball. I did some investigating and spoke to many of the older black men who hung out at barbershops and played dominos on street corners, asking them all sorts of questions about Negro baseball. I knew from my experiences growing up in the South that if I wanted to know anything about life, I had to ask the older folks. No one tells a story like an old black man, "the old-timers" who have seen it all.

They were more than happy to share their wisdom with me. I got an education on some of the great black players of the Negro Leagues. Their stories seemed like fables; they were so fanciful in nature. Experiences of seeing greats like Satchel Paige, Oscar Charleston, Cool Papa Bell, Josh Gibson, Buck Leonard, Turkey Stearnes, and others rolled out of the mouths of these old men as if they knew each player personally. Legendary teams like the Chicago American Giants, Kansas City Monarchs, Memphis Red Sox, Pittsburgh Crawfords, and Homestead Grays were just as common to these men as teams like the New York Yankees, Boston Red Sox, Chicago Cubs, and Los Angeles Dodgers are to baseball fans nowadays.

The old-timers were also knowledgeable about how the Negro Leagues worked. I was astonished to learn that in Negro baseball a team's roster could change on a dime. Players were often lured away during the season by competing teams offering a better salary. Many of the teams, while barnstorming through towns, were looking for outstanding young talent they could recruit to enhance their ball club. This sounded like a prime opportunity for my burgeoning dreams of becoming a baseball player. One of the more legendary stories around these parts was that of Negro League pitching star Ray Brown, now a Hall of Famer, who had played in and around Dayton for years. Word was the Homestead Grays had snatched him up while he was in college at Wilberforce University, the oldest private black university in America. I thought to myself, *Humph, good enough for Ray Brown, good enough for Bob Motley.*

The only thing he could have possibly had on me was some college education and, from what I had heard, that was certainly not a prerequisite to play baseball in the Negro Leagues. I saw no reason why I couldn't make a squad with a little hard work, practice, and determination.

Over the course of the next few months, as I counted the days until spring rolled around, I spent my few spare moments working to perfect my game. When the weather was good I'd walk over to Ducks or one of the sandlot parks and play with the other boys, or I'd play catch with Burt. When the weather was too cold or rainy we'd play ball indoors on the gym floor at the local YMCA. Ever since my days spent throwing rocks at woodland creatures back in Alabama, I was determined to be a pitcher. So I focused on throwing the ball and neglected swinging the bat. I knew that pitchers were not expected to be great hitters, and since I couldn't hit a lick, I felt that pitching was a safer bet. I told no one of my dream, just in case it backfired on me, but I devoted myself to it and practiced with the utmost determination. I practiced so much in fact that I was supremely confident that when one of the Negro League teams came barnstorming through in the spring that my name would be among those fairytale stories of "local boy makes good."

Sure enough, in the spring of 1941 those familiar placards advertising the barnstorming games were being tacked up all over town. My time had come. The first game advertised pitted the Cleveland Buckeyes against the Detroit Black Sox. The day before the big game, I headed over to Ducks armed with my beloved glove, and waited for one of the teams to arrive for their pregame day practice session. As I watched the Buckeyes' bus roll up to the stadium I was jazzed, and silently thought to myself, *I'm sure I can deal with living in Cleveland.*

As the Cleveland team began readying for practice I approached the manager, Walter Burch, and confidently introduced myself, telling him that I was a pitcher and wanted to try out for his team. Burch—a short, dark-skinned, gruff guy who looked like he hadn't cracked a smile in a century—barely looked at me and without missing a beat said, "Let's see what you got." I couldn't believe my ears. Those were the sweetest words I had ever heard in my life.

Without interrupting the rest of the team's workout, Burch called a player over and told him to grab a mitt to catch me. I assumed it was the team's catcher, but since I got no introduction I didn't know for sure. We stood outside the third-base line, and I began to hurl pitches as quickly and as hard as I could. At this point I didn't know how to throw a curveball or any breaking pitches; I was just throwing fastballs. After about ten minutes the skipper interrupted the session and said, "Alright, young man. You got some pretty good stuff. You work out here with us today and then be back here in the morning around ten o'clock and you can suit up with us." It was just as simple as that—at age 17, I was going to be a Cleveland Buckeye!

Uncle Samuel couldn't believe that his little nephew was going to be a big-league pitcher. "Boy, I didn't know you was that good. I just thought you and Burt were horsing around all this time," he told me. I was determined to make him proud. I could hardly sleep a wink that night, tossing and turning as my mind raced with grandiose visions of being the newly touted Satchel Paige of the Negro Leagues. Tomorrow would be the first real game of my life, and it was with the big boys!

I was at the stadium by 8 a.m., two hours before my call time. I didn't want to take the chance of anything going wrong that day. When the team bus rolled up I felt the butterflies begin to whirl around in the pit of my stomach, but I would not be daunted. Upon seeing me, Burch cracked a wee bit of a smile out of the corner of his mouth and told the equipment manager to get me a uniform. Heading onto the field and into the sunshine, I was suffocated by my thick wool uniform in the 90-degree morning heat. The uniform was about two sizes too big for me, but I didn't care. I was a Buckeye!

As the stands began to fill with spectators, so too did my stomach with more butterflies. But I calmed myself down by the start of the game and was feeling confident up until Burch hustled over to me and said, "Kid, you got the apple today." Translated into layman's terms: "Kid, you're the starting pitcher." Needless to say, the butterflies immediately returned with a vengeance.

I was a total wreck! *What the hell had I gotten myself into?* I wondered. Here I was, suited up for the Negro Leagues, and I had barely played sandlot ball. The wheels began to spin in my mind. I now wondered why some of the other guys I'd been playing with on the lots (who I knew were a lot more polished than I was) had never tried to infiltrate one of these teams. I chalked it up to my gall, and, still fighting my panic, tried blocking everything out of my mind and concentrating on the task at hand. I tried convincing myself that all the fans in the stands would be witnessing the historic debut of a soon-to-be ace pitcher bound for greatness in the Negro Leagues. I began to settle down; I was right where I wanted to be, after all. *If Mama was here she would be mortified, but boy would good ol' Locker Burns get a kick out of this!* I told myself.

A scratchy recording of the National Anthem blared through the stadium's loud speakers, and the umpire shouted, "Play ball!" I trotted onto the field along with my new teammates—none of whom I had yet met. Momentarily, as I stood on the mound, I thought about all of those great black ballplayers who had graced this diamond. Then I snapped back into reality as the first Black Sox batter dug in at the plate. I fidgeted, wound up, reared back, and hurled my fastest fastball. *Whack!*—a line-drive base hit into left field. The second batter dug in, I unleashed another fastball, and, *Whack!*—a monstrous double into right center! The third batter swung at my first offering. *Whack!*—another double! The scoreboard read: Black Sox 2, Buckeyes 0. I couldn't for the life of me figure out what I was doing wrong. After all, I could strike out all the boys on the sandlots. Then I remembered, *Oh yeah, this is not the sandlot!*

Looking back, I don't know what possessed me to think that after only a season of sandlot ball I could possibly be ready for the black major leagues. It just goes to show how naïve I really was. I had only one pitch, an obviously lousy fastball, and knew nothing of a curve, slider, or knuckleball. I guess I can only blame it on the ignorance of my youth.

At any rate, I was able to calm myself down by talking to myself, tuning out the deafening boos that were already raining down from the stands. I was determined to strike out my next opponent, or at least *get him out*. I settled in, wound up, and hurled what I thought was my fastest pitch yet. *Whack!*—a triple off the center-field wall! I had thrown just four pitches, and allowed four hits and three runs with nobody out!

At that point Burch trotted out to the mound. I'll never forget his words as he glared into my eyes: "Boy, I thought you said you could pitch!" He continued to bark at me: "No one else better get another hit off you! You understand me?" Exasperated, the only words I could mutter were, "Yes, sir." The catcher, whose name I never knew, had also come out for the meeting on the mound. Staying behind for a moment after Burch had stormed off, he tried to help calm my flailing nerves, but only made matters worse. "Settle down, settle down, youngster," he counseled. I thought to myself, *What the hell you think I'm trying to do?* Almost babying me, he offered worthless words of encouragement as he pointed to the heart of his mitt, saying, "Hit this glove right here. Nail it right here."

Looking around the field, I could see my other nameless teammates staring at me, angered and in disbelief. It's a lonely feeling out there on the mound when you're getting slaughtered with no hope in sight. Even today I empathize with young pitchers who find themselves in a similar situation. Here I was, given the opportunity of a lifetime, and I was about to blow it. *No, I couldn't. I wouldn't!* I told myself. Determined, I focused on the heart of the catcher's mitt, wound up, reared back, and hurled another smoking Motley fastball. It must have been a floater, because the last thing I saw of the ball was the ass of it flying out of the park at record pace over the left-center-field wall. Black Sox 5, Buckeyes 0.

The moment I turned around from watching the ball sail over the fence, I could see Burch out of the corner of my eye running full steam toward me looking as if he was about to rip my head off. Although he was a good five or six inches shorter than me, he looked like a fire-breathing giant barreling toward me. He was pissed! And I wasn't about to give him an opportunity to kick my ass—I was already deeply humiliated. I bolted past him, ducking and dodging to make sure I was out of arms' length. I ran as fast as I could down the dugout stairs, through the clubhouse, out the stadium gate, and all the way back to my bedroom in Uncle Samuel's house on Reist Avenue. I didn't settle down until my bedroom door was locked behind me. There I sat on my bed, huffing and puffing and incredibly embarrassed, when I realized I was still in the team uniform. I had left my clothes at the stadium, but I was never going to step foot in that joint again.

As I sat on the edge of my bed in a dejected silence all afternoon long, the echoing cheers and jeers of the stadium began to fade from my brain, along with my dream. I was an imposter. In the ensuing weeks, I thought of somehow returning the uniform to the team's office in Cleveland via mail, but was just too mortified to remind them of my existence. Instead, I tossed the uniform, along with my beloved glove, into the nearest city dumpster. Bob Motley would never be a star baseball player in the Negro Leagues.

WAR! DECEMBER 7, 1941—"the day that will live on in infamy." It was a scary time for the whole country, and my life was about to change dramatically.

By now, a year and a half after my failed tryout with the Buckeyes, I was done licking my wounds and now trying to figure out what to do with the rest of my life. Thankfully, very little was ever mentioned about my less than stellar pitching debut by my family and friends, so I was spared too much additional humiliation. At the time I wasn't much of a social person, so I just kept a low public profile by going about my regular work routine. When I did have to venture out among people, I always made sure I tilted my fedora to cover as much of my face as possible. I had to be incognito so that anyone who was at that miserable game couldn't recognize me. I even went through the trouble of finding a new barbershop to ensure my anonymity amongst the gossipmongers those establishments seem to attract. Sometimes when I'd walk down the street, I'd sense some whispers, stares, and chuckles from people in my immediate neighborhood. But maybe I was just being paranoid.

I needed a new life, an opportunity to start from scratch. With the war raging, several of my buddies had decided that they were going to enlist in the Armed Forces. I had never given any thought to serving in the military. As far as I was concerned, pimping out prostitutes to soldiers at the Jefferson Davis Hotel was as close as I'd ever get to the military. I never pictured myself as a military man.

Back in those days, the black community knew that the white military establishment possessed a fear of "racial contamination."

Even though black soldiers served bravely and died in battle, our contributions to the war effort were considered neither necessary nor significant. Blacks were not thought to be able-bodied or intelligent enough to meet the demands of combat, so I didn't give serving in the military much thought until meeting a co-worker named Willie Allen.

Willie was a highly intelligent young black man, a few years my senior, who had graduated from Ohio State University. I was totally impressed with his credentials, considering at 19 years old I still didn't even have a high school degree. Although he was not employed by the military, he should have been; Willie was a one-man recruiting service who preached daily that we "young Negro men need to be bold, brave, and brash." Willie encouraged us to seriously consider enlisting in the Armed Forces. A magician with words, he made the military sound like a fanciful wonderland. The perks were all great: a good salary, a pension, a GI loan that would lead to an education, and a chance to see the world. The thought of coming home in a body bag never even crossed my mind while listening to Willie's pitch.

Willie had an extremely radical view of how American society treated its black citizens. He spoke with the fervor of a black Southern Baptist preacher: "The North ain't that much different from the South. The honkies up here won't call you a nigga to your face, but they'll lynch your ass just the same." He convinced many of us that we would be making a tremendous contribution to black society by serving in the military, proving to whites that blacks were capable of doing everything the white man could do. I agreed.

Willie was a mentor and an inspirational force that came along at a time when my confidence was shaken and I had no vision for my future. His passion and pride were things I yearned for myself, and the Armed Forces seemed like a good place to start. So in the spring of 1943, my brother William accompanied me to the Dayton Court House, and on May 21, 1943, I enlisted as a member of the United States Marine Corp.

4

DUTY LEADS TO PASSION

"The cultural dynamic began to change, and I'm proud to say it was
the military and baseball that started that change. . . .
They were the first two great Civil Rights actions."

* Colin Powell *

A FEW DAYS AFTER ENLISTING in the Marines, I boarded a
troop truck in Dayton along with other black volunteers from all over
Ohio. We were hauled off like cattle to our new home and training
facility at Camp Lejeune, North Carolina. Located in the swampy,
wooded, coastal plains of North Carolina near the city of Jacksonville,
Camp Lejeune was and still is one of the primary Marine operations
serving the nation.

Running through a section of the camp is the New River.
During World War II, the river served as the dividing line for
black and white soldiers. The black soldiers were designated to an
area known as Montford Point. Across the banks of the river the
white soldiers were based in the main camp. Blacks were not
allowed to set foot onto the grounds at Camp Lejeune unless

accompanied by a white soldier. My new rules were made clear, although the reasoning made little sense. Black and white soldiers could die together, but God forbid they have a chance to live together.

Our barracks at Montford Point were nothing more than oversized steel-framed tents called Quonset huts. They were durable and served their purpose, but it was hardly a room at the Ritz. The white soldiers' living quarters, although still not luxurious, were unquestionably more humane than ours. I can't help but think the quality of their food rations must have been better than ours as well.

When I joined, the military had recently set a quota on the number of Negroes it would allow into the Marines. Later there would be similar quotas in workplaces throughout the country, and some even said in Major League Baseball as well. I was one of the first black Marines in the history of this country. Before my enlistment, blacks had served in other branches of the Army and Navy, but the Marines and Air Force were considered exclusive groups. At the time I was unaware of the significance of this historic venture by the military. Now, looking back, becoming a Marine is one of my proudest accomplishments.

Oddly enough, it was first lady Eleanor Roosevelt who convinced her husband Franklin to sign an Executive Order prohibiting racial discrimination by government agencies, which finally opened the doors for all Americans to serve in all branches of the military. Before then there was a clause excluding Negroes, Mulattos, and Indians from serving. Although I was not politically minded or active in those days, I often regarded Eleanor Roosevelt as a great woman for her outspokenness on issues of discrimination. She was a hero of sorts in the black community. We all spoke of her with great respect. I would gain even more respect for her in subsequent years as she began to speak out about discrimination in the national pastime.

Upon arrival at Camp Lejeune I was met by a white commanding officer (there were no black officers at the time) and assigned to my division as Private Motley. In those days the lower class soldiers were referred to as "buck privates." My buck private status would not last long. A couple of weeks into boot camp I had already begun to climb the ranks. One of the white drill instructors asked the privates if anyone wanted to take over the group and become platoon leader. The words had barely gotten out of his mouth when I enthusiastically raised my hand and said, "I do!" In that instant, Private Motley became Private *First Class* Motley, platoon leader, which earned me one stripe on my uniform.

I loved the feeling of importance I had as platoon leader. Standing in front of all those tough soldiers and being able to command respect and give directions was empowering. I didn't realize it at the time, but that feeling of being in control was the precursor to my love for umpiring.

In addition to sporting activities, there were also numerous talent shows, dances, and other social activities to keep us busy in our downtime. A few professional black bands performed for us, but mostly the black military band—which featured prominent musicians who had performed with greats like Count Basie and Cab Calloway—had the honor of entertaining us, much to our delight. Although I wasn't much of a dancer or partier, I remember quite distinctly bopping to the music of bandleader Bobby Troup on one particular evening. Lieutenant Troup was a white officer with a black backing band. That sticks out in my mind because it was the first time I had seen an integrated band. Hell, it was the first time I had ever seen black and white men do much of anything together. There, for the first time in my 19 years of living, I saw no racism, no barriers, and no segregation. And let me tell you, we partied that night! Years later I recalled Bobby Troup's name when his classic jazz composition "Route 66" was made famous by the smooth and elegant Nat King Cole.

INITIALLY, MY GOAL WAS to become a commissioned officer. I knew I had the drive and the guts, but I lacked one essential requirement—a high school diploma. With that goal off limits I had to choose another route in order to make my presence known, so I chose to become a military policeman (MP). I took my job as an MP very seriously. So serious in fact, that within weeks of starting my new gig, I had earned the nickname "Dick Tracy" from my fellow soldiers.

I was a mean son of a bitch. I took a no-nonsense attitude when it came to my job, making sure that the soldiers behaved like soldiers were supposed to behave—like gentlemen. When on duty I carried myself with a humorless rigidity that was meant to intimidate the toughest ruffian. When the guys got too rowdy, I'd take control. With billy club in hand and my .45 caliber pistol snuggled in the holster on my hip, I'd patrol the aisles of our makeshift movie theater making sure everyone was on good behavior. When a soldier caused too much of a disturbance and didn't pipe down after I warned him, I'd first jab him in the ribs with my billy club. If he didn't quiet down at that point, I'd drag him outside and beat the crap out of him. It wasn't pretty to watch, but it kept the soldiers in line, which is exactly what my superiors told me to do.

One of my favorite activities was to wait just inside the entrance to Montford Point for drunken soldiers to come back to camp after a night on the town. Once the soldier stumbled onto the grounds, I'd question him about his activities of the night. If I didn't like his answer or attitude, and smelled what I felt was too much liquor on his breath, I'd take him into the shower and turn freezing cold water on him to sober him up. Much to my delight, he'd scream bloody murder as the frigid water beat down on his head.

As cruel as it sounds now, I was young and full of piss and vinegar. For all of my ass-whooping escapades I never got into any trouble with the higher officials, because technically I was doing my job. That is, until the night I damn near killed a man. I had gone into the town of Jacksonville, about ten miles from camp, with one of my fellow MP officers to have what I had planned to be a rare relaxing evening. Neither of us were drinkers, but we decided to go to a local establishment that the soldiers frequented. The second I entered the bar, one of the many inebriated black soldiers spotted me and shouted, "Hey—there's Dick Tracy! Black motherfucker!" I didn't answer him. His buddy jumped in "Yeah, Dick Tracy, you son of a bitch. You off duty now, nigga! We gonna beat the shit out of yo' black ass." Hoping to avoid a confrontation, again, I was silent. Finally, a third guy, Art "Booger Bear" Stewart, got up in my face. "We gonna take you on," he said, taunting me. I calmly replied, "If you do, you'll be sorry."

That's when all hell broke loose. Out of the corner of my eye I saw a fist coming at me. I ducked just in time, but the fight was on! In true Dick Tracy form I positioned myself with my back up against the bar so that I could have a good vantage point of my attackers. I had the foresight to grab two beer bottles off the bar and smack them into each other, arming myself with a sharp weapon in each hand. I challenged them, shouting, "Come on if you want to!" And they came!

My buddy and a few other soldiers jumped in to try to break up the action, but it was already too late. I thought to myself, *I may go down, but one of you bastards is going down with me.* Every time one of them lunged at me I went at him with the broken beer bottles. As the fighting intensified, I stayed on Booger Bear Stewart and cut him like a loaf of bread on a plate. By now my instincts had kicked into high gear, telling me to "kill or be killed," which is how every soldier is conditioned for battle. Rage and fear had taken me over so completely that I didn't realize until the fight was finally broken up that I had been badly injured. I had a deep gash on my right shoulder and scratches all over my body. The doctor told me that I was a lucky man, because if the gash had been a fourth of an inch to the left it would had ruptured my jugular and I would have likely bled to death. Although the other two soldiers escaped relatively unharmed, the man I had concentrated on—Stewart—fared far worse than I had: he was laying on his deathbed a few beds down from me in the military hospital. It was time to face my consequences.

Colonel Samuel Woods was an even-tempered man whom we all had a profound respect for. When he addressed a soldier he looked him right in his eyes like a psychic reading a man's soul. Around camp, some referred to him as "The Great White Father," because he was always concerned about the well being and fair treatment of black soldiers. I had only seen him from a distance, and had always hoped to have a chance to meet him face to face—but certainly not under these circumstances.

Although we all knew him to be kind and generous, it was also well known that Colonel Woods could be quick to anger when unpleased and provoked. Such was the case when I was called into his office after he had learned of the barroom incident. The meeting didn't last long, but it felt like an eternity. Sweating profusely, I explained to him what had happened as he listened intently. When I finished, he spoke in a sobering tone. "Young man," he said, "if your fellow soldier dies, I will see to it personally that you face a court martial." Those were the most dreadful words I had ever heard.

After I was released from the hospital, I went back to the infirmary on a daily basis to peek in on the debilitated soldier to make sure he was still alive. I had never prayed so hard in all my life. Thankfully, Stewart was spared, as was I. Because it was an act of self-defense, I didn't have to do any time, nor was I charged with any criminal act. I was, however, stripped of my beloved military police moniker and demoted to platoon sergeant. But I could accept that fate. I had learned an invaluable lesson: I should have been mentally preparing to fight the real enemy that was awaiting me many miles from home, not my black brothers who would be fighting alongside me. I also learned that there was more to life than trying to be a badass.

By now word had spread around camp that "Dick Tracy" had gotten into a fight and had almost killed another soldier. I had been a known figure before, but now I was notorious. Soon, there was a bounty on my black ass. On the eve before the 51st Infantry was to ship off to battle, some fellow soldiers who were friends with Stewart decided that I would be a dead man before they set sail to the backwaters of the Pacific. Fortunately, word got back to me that I was a wanted man, so I had a window of time that allowed me to save myself.

At sunset, my fellow fighters began shooting up the entire camp, hunting for Dick Tracy. It was like watching the Klan driving past my house on Buttermilk Road all those years ago. From sundown to sun up they roamed the camp, determined to leave my corpse behind. However, they weren't counting on my cleverness; I was one step ahead of them. Actually, I was one step *below* them. I had found my safe haven underneath the steps leading up to one of the barracks. I was under foot the entire time, watching the soldiers scour the site looking for me. I can laugh about it now, but in the heat of the moment I shivered with fear. With each rifle blast, I saw my life flash before my eyes. The manhunt lasted about six hours, until the boys of the 51st Infantry finally set sail around five o'clock in the morning. I have never been so happy to see the sun rise.

A few weeks later I was well and strong enough to get back to the matters at hand, preparing to do battle. I set sail with the 2nd Division of the 52nd Infantry Regiment of the United States

Marine Corps. I was finally heading to battle against the *real* enemy thousands of miles from home.

IT'S AN OLD, BUT TRUE, CLICHÉ: war is hell! It is treacherous, unforgiving, and downright inhumane. If you've never served in the military or fought in combat then you can't possibly imagine the level of conflict that occurs in your soul when you have to take the life of another human designated as the enemy. Hearing the horrific cries of the wounded and seeing death up close and personal takes years to get over—and some never do.

In the case of World War II, the battle for the good of the world was a necessity. If I had to do it all over again, I would enlist a second time. Not so much for the sake of shooting a gun, throwing a hand grenade, stabbing someone, or taking a life, but because oddly enough it was due to my service that I discovered my life's passion, umpiring.

My outfit was the third wave of American soldiers to invade the Japanese island of Okinawa. The first and second waves were entirely wiped out. As my black company prepared to storm the island, we were all grappling with the knowledge that we probably wouldn't survive, either. We were aware that the military had set us up to be a "death squad." Black soldiers were always put on the front lines, used as pawns to pave the way for the white soldiers, who were waiting to follow after we had cleared the way. This is not to say that there were not numerous casualties among white soldiers—that much is a given—but the percentage of black Marines killed in World War II is quite disproportionate to that of white Marines. Black companies simply lost a greater number of their troops than white companies. My company suffered many fatalities as well. Those of us who only sustained injuries were the lucky ones.

In one particular battle after my company established our beachhead on Okinawa, we began a fiercely fought sequence with the Japanese regime. Armed with my rifle, bayonet, hand grenades, gas mask, food rations, and about 50 pounds of ammunition, I was ready for battle. Or so I thought. With bullets flying and bombs dropping all around, I crawled into a foxhole to reload my ammunition. One of the initial lessons I was taught in basic training is that when climbing out of a foxhole, I should never stick my head out first. Instead, I was taught to always dangle a foot out first, to be on the safe side in case of errant gunfire or a sniper. Better to get shot in the foot rather than the head—a lesson that saved my life.

After reloading, I lifted my foot from the foxhole to insure a clear pathway. The first time, the coast was clear. Just as I started to climb out, my inner voice told me, *Uh-uh, stick your foot out again.* All of sudden, *pow!* A pain shot through my right foot that was so intense I expected to see the face of St. Peter before me. I had been shot. I sunk back into the foxhole, writhing in pain for what seemed like a lifetime. Finally, I was rescued and carried back to the ship. For my heroism I would later receive a much beloved Purple Heart. But at that moment, as I was transported to the hospital, I simply thanked God that I didn't get my brains blown out.

Incapacitated and lying in that hospital bed during my recuperating period, I was bored beyond belief and mad as hell. The throbbing pain in my foot didn't help matters. One afternoon, when I started to feel a bit stronger, I hobbled outside to get some fresh air. Off in the distance I could hear the familiar sounds of a bat striking a ball, and the popping of mitts. Curious, I made my way through the thick brush until I reached an open field where soldiers were playing a baseball game. Some of the soldiers like me had been injured and were rehabilitating, while others were healthy and simply waiting for assignment. As I watched from a distance, that old yearning returned.

Back in my hospital bed I talked myself out of ever donning a glove again, but I couldn't shake my desire to be a part of the game. Then, as if ol' Locker Burns was whispering in my ear, I remembered "the silent man of the diamond." It hit me like a ton of bricks—I could umpire! In a flash, I jumped out of bed so quickly that I forgot about the gaping hole in my foot. The only thing that mattered to me was getting back to that field. I introduced myself to the players and volunteered to call balls and strikes. After the game was over, no one complained about my umpiring, so I figured I must have done a pretty good job despite the fact that I didn't really know what I was doing.

Unlike playing the game, umpiring was a natural fit for me. Everything about it jived with my personality. I could be as boisterous, flamboyant, or animated as I wanted. There were no rules for the umpire. I could be goofy and silly or I could be serious and strict; the only real requirement was to be fair and call a play as accurately as possible. That I could do.

Over the next month I umpired every pickup game that was played. After learning about another nearby camp where soldiers were also playing, I began making the trek over there as well. I couldn't get enough baseball: "the silent man" was the perfect role for me. Here in the middle of the war of wars I developed a new skill and passion, one that would sustain me for the rest of my life. Who would have ever thought that was possible?

Although most of the Marines were just average in their athletic skills, there were occasions when someone's ability stood out. Such was the case with two guys who eventually graduated to Negro League ball, Ernest Burke and Bill Greason. Burke was a tall bruiser of a guy, and I immediately noticed his skill with the bat. Whereas most of the guys were playing just to pass the time and forget about the stresses of war, Burke played with a competitive edge that set him apart. His talents later carried him into the Negro

Leagues, where he pitched and played outfield for the Baltimore Elite Giants. Although our paths never crossed after military service, I'm sure he was one of those unsung heroes who brought a lot of excitement to those who got a chance to see him play. Greason, meanwhile, was a solid right-hand pitcher who later spent some time with the Birmingham Black Barons organization. After I graduated to the Negro Leagues a few years later, I recognized Bill immediately as I boarded a bus with the Black Barons on one of my many barnstorming trips. He later became one of the many Negro League players to be drafted by a major league club, and appeared in a few games for the St. Louis Cardinals. Although he never became a household name, he was truly one of those gifted players that the Negro League was blessed to call its own.

There is one soldier whom I think of often, even now some 60 years later. This kid—whom we just called "Young Blood," never knowing his real name—was one of the best ballplayers I have ever seen. He was almost childlike in demeanor, but his maturity for a baseball player was well beyond his years. He had the potential to be a superstar in the Negro Leagues and probably beyond thanks to his raw power with the bat, his talent with the glove, and his speed on the basepaths. His rocking batting stance and smooth, quick swing reminds me today of Ken Griffey, Jr.

Young Blood was a soft-spoken kid who never had much to say. He let his bat do his talking. But when he did speak his words were always the same: "When I get back home my mama's gonna be proud of me, 'cause I'm gonna be a man!" If I heard him say that once I heard him say it a hundred times. Unfortunately, Young Blood didn't make it back home or to the Negro Leagues. As he was waiting in the chow line only a couple people in front of me, he caught a Japanese sniper's bullet right in the head.

That was the saddest day of my entire military service.

NOT COUNTING ANY NEAR-DEATH EXPERIENCES in the chow line, I was enjoying being out of harm's way and loving my daily dose of umpiring. I had a routine down pat that ensured that I'd be laid up for a good while. Every day when the nurse came by to check up on me, I always complained that my foot, leg, and now head were aching. Humphrey Bogart had nothing on me with the daily Oscar-winning performances I was delivering. The nurse had no reason not to believe me, so she continued pumping me with aspirin, feeling sorry for this sickly, incapacitated solider. The moment she was done with her rounds, I'd slip out the back of the hospital and make a beeline for the ball field to indulge my newfound passion.

Learning a new skill wasn't a bad trade off for nearly having my foot blown off. But like all good things, my little affair with the ball diamond had to come to an end. My brother James was serving in the Army and had somehow heard through the grapevine that I had been injured. Being a good big brother, he found out where I was and came to check on me. When he couldn't find me in the hospital he grew concerned and asked the nurse about my condition. She told him, "Oh, Motley's fine, getting stronger every day. He's around here somewhere." With that, they began to look for me. The nurse saw firsthand that I was much better than I had been letting on when she discovered me behind the plate on the ball field. The very next day, I found myself on a ship headed back into battle. It was good to see my brother, and I appreciated his concern, but damn if he didn't mess up my good thing!

Back on the battlefield in Saipan, Tinian, and Guam I would endure many more harrowing experiences, the most terrifying of which was being surrounded by Japanese soldiers in a barrage of gunfire and grenade and mortar shell explosions. The Japanese were in heavy pursuit of my squadron in a battle we were losing badly. As a matter of fact, more than half of my company was killed in that skirmish. There were so many dead bodies lying around they could have covered the playing field of any major league ballpark with the corpses.

As my surviving comrades and I retreated, the pounding of my heart intensified to the point that I could hardly breathe. The sound of gunfire and explosions was deafening, and I could barely see from the spray of dirt and blood that was stinging my eyes. Knowing the Japanese soldiers were minutes from capturing or killing the rest of us, our company scattered in a panic, every man for himself. While some of our troops fled into the jungles of the island, I fell to the ground along with a few others and began covering myself with the mangled, entangled bodies of dead soldiers, both American and Japanese. I pulled at least three or four bodies on top of me, hoping that my best defense was to play dead.

Lying under the heaviness of all that dead weight was almost suffocating. With a mix of warm and cold blood spilling into my eyes, nose, and mouth, I laid motionless beneath the rubble of corpses as my pursuers trampled over me, stabbing and thrashing body after body with bayonets to ensure that there were no survivors. I heard the groans and screams of my fellow soldiers as they were discovered alive and then brutally slaughtered, some within feet of where I was buried. Finally, after what seemed like an eternity, the Japanese soldiers scampered on, and the few of us who had survived breathed quiet sighs of relief. We lay perfectly still until we were confident the coast was clear. When the time came, we retreated back to the American forces, looking over our shoulder at every turn. I'd been through some hell before, but that was as close to death as I ever cared to be.

August 15, 1945, marked "V-J Day," the surrender of Japan and the winding down of a hard-fought, bloody battle. The news was welcomed by the world at large, but no one was happier about it than us weary soldiers. When the news finally reached us we celebrated for days on end. Later, on February 1, 1946, I would receive my honorable discharge from military service. I had given America two and a half years of intense service, and the country still had not granted full rights to me or my black brethren. But we were all hopeful that life would somehow be better.

That hope turned to a promise when further good news followed a short time later. While spending what would be my final days in Saipan, I received word through others in camp that a young Negro baseball player named Jackie Robinson—a man who had also served his country during World War II, although he did not see combat—had signed a major league contract with the Brooklyn Dodgers. Those surviving black soldiers in my company rejoiced with me at the news. We *never* thought we'd live to see the day when a black man would be admitted into the major leagues. We hooted and howled something fierce that day. That historic event served as a signal that things would indeed be different back home. Equality was within our reach. After all, if a black man could integrate the great American pastime, anything seemed possible.

Sailing home was a sweet journey. For the first time in a long while, I relaxed and simply enjoyed being alive. Although "Young Blood" had not made it back with us, I prayed silently that his soul would be blessed to know that his experience *had* made him a man, just as it had for all of us who served in the war. I also prayed that his mother was indeed proud of his sacrifice, as I knew my own mother would be of mine.

I had come a long way from kicking soldiers' butts and being so full of myself that I thought the universe centered around me. For the first in my life I had developed a camaraderie with, and a respect and love for, a group of men who had become like brothers to me. We had carried out our mission and defeated a cunning and dangerous enemy, all the while earning the respect of the white military establishment as viable soldiers and equal human beings. Yes, life *would* be better back home.

Even now, I become filled with emotion when I think about seeing the Golden Gate Bridge in the distance as our ship sailed into the San Francisco harbor. It was a welcome sight for sure. For most people, the Statue of Liberty is what comes to mind when they think of symbols that represent America and all her promise. For me, it was and still is that golden deity shimmering majestically in the Pacific sun that saluted this black Marine as he returned to a land that had long ago promised that *all* men are created equal.

5

PERSISTENCE PAYS OFF

"Bob Motley was one of our best umpires. He was strict and didn't take no mess. But he was fair, consistent, and a hell of a showman!"
* Bob Scott, New York Black Yankees *

AFTER THE WAR, I returned to Anniston, Alabama, to see Mama and to retrieve the thousands of dollars in military earnings I had sent home for her to hold for me. Upon arrival, Mama informed me that she had needed my money to support herself—all that was left was about $700. I was devastated, but I didn't let it show.

Seven hundred dollars was still enough to buy myself a used automobile and set my plan in motion to return to Dayton as soon as possible. My brother James, who had come back home from the war shortly before me, begged me to first give him a lift to Kansas City, Missouri, to see our sister Geraldine, who had moved there with her new husband. To me, Kansas City was some far-off land in the wild, wild west. While I wanted to see my favorite sibling, Geraldine, I really had no interest in going there at all. Furthermore, it was a complete detour from my direct route to Dayton, and I was anxious to get back to Uncle Samuel and my family up north. But when James offered to buy all the gas and food for my journey, I changed my tune.

Boy am I glad I did. Once we arrived in Kansas City and I got a taste of the town, I didn't give another thought to returning to Dayton. Kansas City was my new home. It had the sophistication, culture, and energy of Dayton—times ten. Jobs, nightlife, activities, a thriving black community, delicious bar-b-que, beautiful women, and a professional black baseball team—the world-famous Kansas City Monarchs. I was in heaven!

I had first heard about the Monarchs from Locker Burns, who always referred to them as "the New York Yankees of the Negro Leagues." The Monarchs ruled black baseball in the Midwest. As one of the first teams founded during the inception of the Negro Leagues in 1920, the Monarchs boasted a highly successful franchise, which had won several world championships and featured some of the best players to ever play the game of baseball.

When I arrived in Kansas City in the spring of 1946, the Monarchs were stocked full of some of the league's best-known talent. Even though Jackie Robinson, a former Monarch, was already in the Brooklyn Dodgers minor league system in Montreal, Quebec, and was about to make history, the Monarchs roster read like a who's who of Negro League stars: Clifford "Connie" Johnson, Jimmy "Lefty" LaMarque, Othello "Chico" Renfroe, Buck O'Neil, Hilton Smith, Ted Strong, Earl Taborn, Satchel Paige, and the absolute best player I have ever seen don a baseball uniform, Willard Brown.

Among the first things I did after arriving in Kansas City was to make my way over to Blues Stadium, which was a stone's throw away from my sister's house. The old stadium stood proudly at the corner of 22nd and Brooklyn Avenue, and like most major-league stadiums of the time, it was in the heart of the black community.

Later in my career, I had the opportunity to umpire in many of the great stadiums of the day, including South Side Park, Comiskey Park, and Wrigley Field in Chicago; Crosley Field in Cincinnati; Westport Stadium in Baltimore: Briggs Stadium in Detroit; Ponce de Leon Park in Atlanta; Ruppert Stadium in Newark; Martin Stadium in Memphis; Forbes Field in Pittsburgh; Engel Stadium in Chattanooga; Wilson Park in Nashville; Griffith Stadium in Washington, D.C.; and the only still-standing chestnut from the era, Rickwood Field in Birmingham. Every one of those ballparks possessed a living, breathing character all its own.

As great as each of those ballparks were, however, none was as special to me as my beloved Blues Stadium. I've often joked that I knew that stadium better than I knew myself, and at times it was somewhat true. Since I umpired the majority of my games there, I was more familiar with that stadium than any other piece of real estate on the planet. Its massive dimensions—350 feet down the left-field line, 421 feet in center, and 347 feet down the right-field line—gave power hitters nightmares, although I did see some awesome slugfests in that park.

Initially named Muehlebach Field when it was built in 1923, and later renamed Municipal Stadium in the mid-1950s, Blues Stadium was the first bona fide professional ballpark I ever stepped foot in. At four times the size of Ducks Ballpark in Dayton, it held a whopping 20,000 people. The stadium needed all that seating not only for Monarchs games, but also because it hosted the Kansas City Blues, the Yankees' minor-league affiliate from 1923 to 1954.

In terms of historical importance, Blues Stadium was second only to Yankee Stadium, as far as I was concerned. Its field had been graced by the presence of every imaginable Negro League star from the 1920s onward. It was also the stadium where Lou Gehrig played his very last game in an exhibition contest in 1939. It's where "the mighty Babe" Ruth couldn't buy a hit off Negro League fireballer Wilbur "Bullet Joe" Rogan in a 1922 exhibition game, until his final at-bat when Rogan lobbed one up to the plate to allow Ruth a chance to crush the ball over the wall just to satisfy fans. It's the stadium where minor leaguers Mickey Mantle, Roger Maris, and Yogi Berra honed their craft as Yankee farm hands before becoming big league legends. It's the stadium where Jackie Robinson donned a Monarchs uniform for a season before becoming an American sports and civil rights icon. And it's the same stadium where I made my professional umpiring debut and called balls and strikes for the legendary Satchel Paige.

I treasured the old stadium and miss it terribly. In the mid-1970s, I campaigned tirelessly along with a few other local businessmen to save the old girl from the wrecking ball, but we were not successful. The day of the demolition I parked alongside Interstate 70 and watched a part of my life being wiped away, plank by plank, bleacher by bleacher. As usual, progress won out; Blues Stadium, along with its cherished history, was demolished in 1976.

Seeing the Monarchs play for the first time at the stadium provided me with an introduction to the true greatness of the Negro Leagues. I had previously only seen a couple exhibition barnstorming games in Dayton. Those were terrific, but seeing official league games that counted in the win-loss column was a whole new ballgame.

My arrival in Kansas City in 1946 came at an exciting time for black baseball in the town, as the Monarchs advanced to the Negro League World Series that year against a hot contender from the East, the Newark Eagles. Run by powerhouse owners Abe and Effa Manley (the latter a Hall of Fame Inductee), the Eagles were another winning franchise whose roster included future Hall of Famers Monte Irvin, Biz Mackey, Leon Day, and

Larry Doby. The three exhilarating Negro League World Series games that were played in Kansas City were major events for the city, which only fanned the flame of my desire to be in "the bigs." Though the Monarchs succumbed to the powerful Eagles in Game 7 of the series, it was a tremendous year for the local team. Its impact on black community pride in and around Kansas City was palpable.

I landed a new job as a janitor at General Motors shortly after moving to Kansas City, but I was still itching to be involved at some level in baseball. Every day I waited impatiently for the two o'clock bell to ring, which signaled the end of my work shift, so that I could head over to the Parade Park ball field at 18th and The Paseo in Kansas City's now "historic district." I'd umpire amateur game after game, sometimes staying until it was almost time to go to work again the following day. Taking my craft ever more seriously, I found a local sporting goods store and invested in a breast protector, facemask, shin guards, shoes, and an umpire rulebook. I was committed to making this happen, to *be* an umpire. So committed, in fact, that the rulebook was actually the first book I ever read cover to cover. And quite honestly, I haven't read that many more since. I was obsessed with the intricacies of baseball, so fascinated by the rules that I tried to commit every line of that book to memory. During my shifts at GM while mopping floors and scrubbing down walls, I'd repeat rule after rule in my mind, testing myself. God forbid if any of my co-workers ever saw me muttering to myself. But it kept me focused on achieving my dream.

While Jackie Robinson was tearing up the majors as a rookie in 1947, I was keeping tabs on his every accomplishment. As I checked his daily box scores and read every article I could find that was written about him, Jackie became the standard of how I wanted to live my life. As I discovered more about his educational and military background, I became motivated to better myself. Somehow between my time spent at work and the sandlots, I found the time to go back to school to get my high school diploma. Proudly, I graduated from Kansas City's all-black Lincoln High School at the ripe old age of 24.

Jackie's feat was something I never took for granted. As tough as the road to the majors had been for him, I knew that other doors would eventually have to be opened to blacks in baseball. That meant that maybe someday soon a black umpire could make his mark in the major leagues. I wanted to be that man, to follow in Jackie's footsteps and do some barrier-breaking of my own as an umpire.

Knowing that Jackie's journey had been a methodical one, I decided not to rush my umpiring dream the way I had rushed my pitching aspirations in my failed tryout for the Cleveland Buckeyes. Instead, I chose to continue developing my skills as an umpire on the amateur level in Kansas City's Ban Johnson League, a prestigious amateur league that had been around since 1927. It was a great training ground for both players and umpires looking to hone their skills while in the company of other likeminded people. Several players who would later go on to become major leaguers cut their teeth in the Ban Johnson League, including Ray Sadecki, Lee Stevens, Rick Sutcliffe, Kevin Young, David Cone, and Frank White.

Even though Kansas City was ripe with its share of racial issues in 1947, I experienced little or no resistance when I entered the Ban Johnson League as its first black umpire that year. Umpiring for the league meant spending most of my free time on diamonds like Parade Park, which was my favorite of Kansas City's amateur fields because it sat in the shadow of Blues Stadium. For as much as I was enjoying umpiring in those amateur games, I had my sights set on that glorious 20,000-seater up on the hill just five short blocks away.

THE SPRING OF 1948 couldn't come fast enough. After getting through my first season of amateur-level baseball I was feeling more confident about my abilities as an umpire. I was eager to take my newfound talent to the next level. Somehow, some way, Bob Motley was going to make his umpiring debut in the Negro Leagues. I had no contacts, no contracts, and no plan—just the desire and determination.

When the first game of the '48 season arrived for the Monarchs, I showed up in the parking lot of Blues Stadium with my breast protector, facemask, shin guards, shoes, and rulebook in hand and a dream in my heart. Like I had done when I tried out with the Buckeyes years earlier, I made my way over to the stadium hours before game time and waited; however, this time I wasn't awaiting the team's arrival, but rather the umpires'. After a long while, three gentlemen approached the stadium entrance. Two of the three I recognized as umpires from watching the Monarchs over the previous two seasons. The third man I recognized as former Monarchs player and manager Frank Duncan, who was carrying his own umpire gear.

I introduced myself and told them of my desire to become an umpire, shamelessly begging them to give me a shot. Duncan spoke up first: "Kid, you don't know nothing about umpiring." One of the other gentlemen, Sylvester "Seal" Vaughn, blurted, "Boy, how old is you? You ain't old enough to keep up with us. We's professionals!" I had my story ready and spoke passionately, telling them of my experiences umpiring in the sandlots around Kansas City, the Ban Johnson League, and overseas in the military. To make my credentials sound even more impressive, I stretched the truth, claiming I had also umpired in Dayton and Alabama. To my astonishment, the veterans didn't seem at all impressed.

After a little back and forth discussion with Duncan and Vaughn, which was going nowhere in my favor, the third umpire spat chaw on the ground and piped in. "Y'all quit hassling this boy," he said. "Kid, we got a full crew. If you're serious, check back with us in a couple of months." And with that, the three umpires turned and entered the stadium, leaving me on the outside looking in.

A couple of months sounded like a lifetime. There was no way in the world I was going to wait that long. So, the very next Sunday I showed up again—same place, same time—with my umpiring gear in hand. As the arbiters approached, they seemed surprised to see me waiting for them. This time, only Duncan addressed me.

"Kid, you back here again?" he asked.

"Yes sir!" I enthusiastically replied, thinking my eagerness would impress.

"Sorry kid, no openings," he quipped without missing a step as the three strode past me.

Once again, I was left behind, disappointed but undaunted. The Monarchs were on the road the following week, but when week four rolled around the team was back in town and I was right back in the stadium parking lot with my umpire gear in tow. Duncan was absolutely astonished (and probably mortified) to see me waiting for them yet again. The others didn't seem to notice or care.

"Alright kid, I ain't making you no promises," Duncan said in his typical gruff voice. "But if you wanna umpire in this here league, you gotta go talk to my boss, Mr. Baird."

That was all I needed to hear. I actually thought that Duncan might have been giving me the runaround, but I did as instructed. The very next afternoon, immediately after getting off work, I drove directly to Mr. Baird's office across the Missouri River on the Kansas side of Kansas City. Thomas Y. Baird was the new, sole owner of the Monarchs, having recently bought out the team's contract from his partner, legendary original owner and recent Hall of Fame inductee J. L. Wilkinson. Baird's office was a tiny, junky space with an entrance through a back alley. Upon entering, again my naiveté surfaced; I assumed that since it was the Negro Leagues that all the team owners must be Negro. Imagine my surprise upon meeting Mr. Baird, an old, white, bespectacled man sitting at his desk behind a mound of paperwork. After I told him the reason for my visit, the first thing he asked me was, "What kind of experience do you have, young man?" My lines by now were well rehearsed, and so I calmly told him the same story that I had told the crotchety umpiring crew upon meeting them at Blues Stadium. Much to my dismay, Baird told me that if I wanted to be an umpire, I would have to deal directly with the Chief Umpire of the Negro American League: Frank Duncan. The same Frank Duncan who had directed me to speak with Baird. "I only sign the paychecks," continued Baird. "Mr. Duncan decides who he wants to hire and work with." The runaround continued.

Duncan had enjoyed a long and distinguished career in the Negro Leagues. As an All-Star catcher he played for several teams throughout his career, but he eventually became known as one of the Monarchs' premiere players. He had done all right for himself financially, as he also owned a very successful taxi stand and tavern in the city. Plus, he was married to popular blues singer Julia Lee. They were the Carole Lombard and Clark Gable of Kansas City's black community. In other words, he was a *somebody*, and I was a *nobody*.

But I was determined to change that. An exasperated Duncan sighed and rolled his eyes when he spotted me yet again in the parking lot. In his familiar harsh voice he blared, "Mr. Baird told me you went to talk to him." "Yes sir," I smiled, before pleading, "Sir, I really want to umpire. I've been working hard, and know I can do it!" Probably sensing that I would not take "no" for an answer, this time he invited me to follow him into the stadium to the umpires' dressing room.

As we sat in the dressing room, Duncan chatted with another umpire, whom I now realized was former Negro League standout

Wilbur "Bullet Joe" Rogan. As the two reminisced about their playing days, not once did they acknowledge me. I stood there, not daring to sit down and assume I could make myself comfortable, fascinated by the tales of baseball royalty, trying to take it all in. Rogan, who is now a Hall of Famer, had been the Monarchs' star right-handed pitcher for nearly 20 years. Possessing a wicked sidearmed delivery and an armory of pitches including a curveball, forkball, and palmball, Rogan was considered by some to be a more accomplished hurler than his renowned teammate Satchel Paige. I personally never got to see Rogan pitch, but his legend was intact in Kansas City and beyond.

He was once a well-rounded and gifted athlete—swinging a big bat and graceful in the outfield; now well into his 50s, the adept umpire moved slowly with a bent back. Still, Rogan was an intimidating presence. With charcoal black skin, always bloodshot eyes, and a brooding presence, he resembled the devil sprung to life; but he was kind and friendly to me. He loved his chewing tobacco and would always spat it out of the corner of his mouth. Although he carried a spit cup with him, he rarely bothered using it. Instead, he'd spit wherever he felt: on the ground, on the side of a wall, on his shoes, on *your* shoes.

In addition to Seal Vaughn, the fourth umpire was Vernon Johnson, a quiet and soft-spoken fellow who often took catnaps before games instead of engaging in banter. Johnson would sometimes show up at the last minute, as the umpires were preparing to head out to the field. Occasionally, he would decide in the sixth or seventh inning that he had stayed long enough, and just leave. He was often off in his own world, probably because he had a little issue with the bottle; on many game days, he reeked of alcohol. I think Duncan only put up with him out of loyalty because Johnson had been around for so long.

Duncan was without a doubt the most personable of the crew. A very gregarious person, he always had something to say, which meant there was rarely a quiet moment in the dressing room. Sometimes when he started to ramble on too much, Rogan would call him a "motor mouth." But that wouldn't stop Duncan. He'd chuckle and keep right on blabbing.

Duncan and Rogan both had a way with foul language. In the armed services, I had been around crude soldiers, but these two old-timers made those soldiers sound like choirboys. Whether talking about a play that had happened during the game or recounting their glory days, Duncan and Rogan were always saying "motherfucker" this or "motherfucker" that. Their talk was racy and crass, but I have to admit, funny as hell!

But as I stood there among the umpiring crew in the bowels of Blues Stadium for the first time, I wasn't thinking of comedy or history—only my future. I didn't get to umpire that day, but my persistence finally paid off one Sunday afternoon shortly thereafter when Johnson failed to show up for the game. Duncan told me, "Kid, you're at third base." Finally, the runaround had ended and I would make my debut as a Negro American League umpire.

The Monarchs were hosting the Memphis Red Sox that day, and our four-man umpire crew consisted of Duncan at home plate, Rogan at first, Vaughn at second, and Bob Motley at third. There I was, seven years after my humiliating tryout as a pitcher, on the turf of a professional ball field—this time wearing a different uniform. The capacity crowd was cheering so loudly that I could barely hear Duncan yell, "Play ball!"

For the first time in my 25 years of living, I knew that I was exactly where I was born to be. I had made it to the big league for coloreds and was about to umpire some of the greatest ball players of our time. This time, I was here to stay.

MY FIRST GAME CAME AND WENT without a hitch. I made a couple of routine calls like an old pro. After the game, Duncan,

Rogan, and Vaughn all complimented me on a job well done. I was pleased as punch. Before he left the dressing room, Duncan turned to me, smiled, and said, "Kid, see you next Sunday."

As I changed back into my street clothes, Tom Baird hobbled into the dressing room on his cane and approached me. "Well young man, I see you got your chance. Welcome to the Negro American League." He informed me that since I was a rookie umpire he would pay me five dollars cash per game. In 1948, five bucks was a lot of money: that kind of change could buy me a couple of meals, gas, and a shirt or two, with enough left over to go toward rent. I was elated!

Some time later, after I had become more confident and established in the league, I mustered up the gumption to ask Mr. Baird for a raise. I thought I was entitled to a bump in pay. But I was brought back down to earth rather quickly when Baird told me concisely and coldly, "You're not a ballplayer. If you don't like the five dollars I'm paying you, go find another job!" Embarrassed and insulted, I never spoke another word to the man. Incidentally, it didn't surprise me one bit when I recently discovered that Negro League historians had uncovered some shocking evidence about Tom Baird. Allegedly, he was a registered member of the Kansas City, Kansas chapter of the Ku Klux Klan. It doesn't quite make sense to me that someone whose entire career centered around Negro baseball could live a double life in his pointed hood and sheet. If true, then I guess his greed for the almighty dollar spoke louder than his grand wizard.

My assignments the first couple of years were sporadic, as I wasn't always needed. Regardless, I'd show up at the ballpark, just in case. I wanted to prove to Duncan and Rogan that I was enthusiastic and hungry for every chance I was given. But just being around the other umpires provided me with a great opportunity to watch and learn from seasoned pros. All the while, I continued umpiring Ban Johnson games and working my day job at General Motors. I was finally worked into the regular rotation during the 1949 season. I assumed third-base duties while Duncan continued to break me in.

Although my fellow umpires had taken me under their wings and allowed me to join their tight circle, they never once gave me any pointers or advice on the art of umpiring. I was on my own I'm sorry to report. Looking back, I'm sure it's because Duncan and Rogan were ballplayers at heart. Their spirit lie in *playing* the game, not observing it. Their faces would light up as they reminisced about their playing days, and umpiring simply didn't have the same effect on them. It was just a way for them to stay active and involved in the game. So what I didn't learn from my rulebook, I had to learn by observing and trusting my instincts.

We always had a four-man crew at Sunday Monarchs games. Duncan was anchored behind home plate. He loved to call balls and strikes and was quite good at it. However, as an aging former catcher, he constantly complained about the failing health of his knees. "Rog'," he would groan to Rogan, "my goddamn knees ain't no fucking good no more. I can't squat worth shit." Rogan never missed a beat, often replying with the same line: "Well, as long as you can squat when you take a shit you're in good shape, Dunc!" We would all howl with laughter at the black version of Laurel & Hardy. But I could tell that Duncan really was in obvious pain.

Rogan was content being at first base because it didn't require him to have to move very far or fast. Vaughn was a pretty weak umpire in my opinion, as he invoked very little emotion in his calls. But at least he was consistent in his routine and never missed a game. I wasn't too interested in remaining at third base. I had my eye on home plate. Every umpire worth his weight longs to be behind the plate calling balls and strikes. The plate umpire is involved in every single play, and as a result controls the game.

Standing around the bases can sometimes get a little monotonous and boring, especially in a pitchers' duel when there are few baserunners. But I was a rookie ump, and I wasn't going to complain. I just loved every minute I spent on the ball field. Eventually, as Duncan's confidence in me grew, he began swapping me with one of the other umps, initially at second with Vaughn, and later with Rogan at first.

My duties as an umpire extended beyond just calling a good game. As the youngest member of the crew, I was assigned the duty of carrying Duncan's breast protector and mask on and off the field before and after the game. He'd say, "Kid,"—they always called me "Kid" because I was so much younger than they were—"make yourself useful and help out the ol' man." I would have gladly carried Duncan on my back if necessary just for the joy of sharing the diamond with him. After all, he had given me the opportunity of a lifetime.

Sometimes before a game, Duncan would have me look the game balls over for cuts, scratches, or grease. In the Negro Leagues we only used about two dozen balls per game, a mix of old and new balls. If need be, we would use a ball until it was close to worn out. The team owners were often penny pinchers and tried to cut costs wherever they could.

As for attire, the umpires in the Negro Leagues had a standard dress code: a black suit, a white shirt, a black bowtie, and black shoes. I took pride in presenting myself as a professional, so I always made sure my clothes were clean, pressed, and neat. Some days the sun's heat would bear down with such intensity that I thought my backside was on fire. It may sound crazy, but on the hottest days, both umpires and ballplayers alike wore long johns under their clothing so that their sweat would dampen their under-clothing and cool them down. Considering the players' uniforms were made entirely of wool, I think we umps had it pretty easy in comparison. I wasn't going to moan about anything—I was having the time of my life. I had come a long way since my days at the sandlots and was beginning to feel like a celebrity, although I quickly realized that the fans actually paid very little attention to the umpires unless one of them made a bum call.

Duncan's knees finally caught up with him toward the end of the '49 season, and he could crouch down no more. Out of respect, I had never suggested taking over for him; he was a workhorse and I knew he had to ride out his time. I just quietly waited, knowing my day was sure to come. The last thing I wanted to appear was overanxious, although I was truly chomping at the bit. Rogan was a senior, so I knew the only squatting he would be doing was on the toilet. And Vaughn had expressed no interest in going behind the plate. That meant the job of home plate umpire would eventually fall in my lap—and it did.

CALLING BALLS AND STRIKES was my dream come true. As I eased into being a home plate umpire I was commanding with my calls but not over the top. I made a conscious effort to be controlled and relatively understated while noting balls and strikes or signaling a strikeout. I didn't want to offend the old guard of Duncan and Rogan by being too showy, lest they think I was trying to upstage them with my youthful energy. Besides, I needed to focus on improving behind the plate.

In the Negro Leagues, the strike zone was more expansive than it is now in the major leagues: it extended from the top of the knees to just under the armpit, whereas now it only goes up to the bottom of the letters. I was a "pitcher's umpire" because I believed in giving the pitcher the benefit of the doubt. And the rules state: if the ball nips any part of that plate within that vertical zone of the body, it's a strike. Now being a pitcher's umpire did get me in trouble with some batters, of course, but I always paid them little mind and just tried to make the best judgment call possible.

When I got totally comfortable in my new role, and after Duncan and Rogan had both retired midway through the 1950 season, I decided it was time to perform. From that point on, I showed up and showed out! I made sure all of my motions were big enough that everyone in the stadium knew what I was calling, adding as much drama to the moment as possible. I leaned out extra far to denote a ball, and I made sure that every time I called a strike my voice carried throughout the stadium— "*S-T-R-R-R-R-I-I-I-I-I-K-E!*" The fans ate it up, and I loved hearing the sound of my voice echoing back at me. I figured the ballplayers were entertaining the crowd with their abilities, so why not the umpires, too? Well at least *this* umpire.

When I was the home plate umpire I'd turn every call into a production. If I was on the base paths and there was a close play, I'd kick one leg up into the air and jerk my arm up and down like a karate chop. If the runner was safe, I'd slide low to the ground, almost doing the splits, with my arms stretched out wide as if about to jump up and take flight. The point was to be dramatic and to make my actions as clear as day; I didn't want any doubters in the stands. I was transforming what Locker Burns had called "the silent man of the diamond" into a memorable part of the game.

After retiring, Rogan and Duncan still came to the park as spectators. They would often make their way to the umpires' dressing room to say hello and tell me what a kick they had gotten watching me perform. "Kid, you something else out there! You givin' them colored folks a show!" Rogan once told me, much to my delight. Duncan praised my efforts as well, saying, "Bob Motley, you got pizzazz!" Because of my respect for those two old-timers, their compliments were really the only validation I needed to affirm that I was on the right path.

One hot summer day while umpiring first base in Blues Stadium, my flashy moves suddenly coalesced into my own signature style. Indianapolis Clowns catcher Sam Hairston bunted a blooper down the third-base line that was scooped up by Monarchs third baseman Herb Souell. As Hairston came barreling toward first base, Souell fired the ball to first, throwing out Hairston by a split second. I got caught up in the thrill of the close play, and my instincts took over: I kicked my leg up a little higher than usual and bellowed, *"O-O-O-O-U-U-U-T-T!"* The fans had come to their feet to applaud the fine play by Souell, and as they started to calm down I heard a lady's voice holler out from the stands, "Do it pretty for me baby!"

I always made a point never to look directly into the stands during the game. Once in a while, I might look around between innings—but never during one. As umpires in the Negro Leagues, we learned to always ignore fans to avoid risking any type of confrontation both on and off the field. We had enough to deal with when it came to the players. But I was struck by this woman's flirtatious voice, and my curiosity got the best of me. I stole a quick glance into the crowd, wondering to myself, *Was she talking to me?* The answer was quite clear when upon catching my eye, the young woman who had obviously blurted out her request winked and waved at me coyly. And she was cute to boot!

I tried to downplay my newfound fan by not acknowledging her with a smile. When the next play happened at first, however, the showman in me came out again. I kicked my leg even higher and twisted my body a bit to put some extra zip in the call. This time she cooed, "Ah, baby that's *pretty.*" With that, I was hooked; it was showboating time from then on! Every time I made a call at first—even if the runner was obviously out by a mile—I found myself leaping, twisting, and turning through the air like Mikhail Baryshnikov gone mad. The crowd went wild, including that pretty little thing up in the fifth row. Just like that, I had my new style.

IT WAS QUITE AN HONOR to hear Duncan tell me on the phone one evening before the start of the 1950 season that he was going to recommend me for the position of "chief umpire" to Tom Baird. Imagine my delight and surprise when the reigning league president, Dr. J. B. Martin of Memphis, Tennessee, called to offer me the job. I accepted, of course.

Martin explained that since Baird was scaling back his involvement in the league, I was to report directly to him. Besides being president and my new boss, J. B. (a dentist), along with his brothers B. B. and W. S. (a dentist and pharmacist, respectively), was also owner of the highly respected Memphis Red Sox team. The brothers had been in the Negro baseball business since the 1920s and were all highly successful businessmen.

Martin invited me to Memphis to discuss my duties as chief umpire. Upon arrival I went directly to his office, where he greeted me with a warm handshake and a pleasant, friendly smile, which was always a permanent fixture on his high-yellow hued face. Immaculate, stately, and organized, his office was like day and night compared to Baird's cluttered space. His attitude was in stark contrast to Baird's as well. Considering that most of the league's umpires were almost twice my age, Martin surprisingly made it clear to me that he was delighted to have a young umpire who was knowledgeable and willing to take on the added responsibilities of chief umpire. Having himself seen me umpire in Kansas City, Martin also complimented me on my skills. My head swelled even more with pride when he told me that Duncan had told him, "There is no one better qualified to fill my shoes as chief umpire than Bob Motley."

After signing my contract and accepting my new post, Martin advised me of my duties. He personally assigned me to various games, gave me a schedule of all league games, and a list of the 40 or so Negro League umpires in the league's ten cities. He further explained that it would be my responsibility to make sure that all umpires were assigned to their games. I would also be in charge of assigning umpires to the barnstorming schedules for the teams I was assigned to travel with.

Best of all, Martin informed me that my salary would be a whopping $300 a month! That was a far cry from the measly five dollars a game I had been getting before. Just like the ballplayers, I would now be paid on the first and 15th of every month. In those days there was no such thing as a meal allowance or per diem for a Negro League umpire, so my salary had to cover all of my living expenses, except for the cost of my lodging on the road.

Dr. Martin certainly took the business of baseball seriously. He explained to me how the leagues had been forced to restructure themselves since the once prosperous Negro National League (which primarily consisted of East coast teams) had folded two years earlier in 1948. By the 1949 season, only the Negro American League was left to hold down the fort of black baseball.

Despite what some people think, the Negro Leagues were always a properly run league. Like the majors, we had a regular game schedule from April to September. We had league presidents, league secretaries, newspaper coverage, spring training, and our own World Series. Our annual All-Star game regularly outdrew the majors' All-Star game by tens of thousands of fans. The most significant difference between Major League Baseball and the Negro Leagues was the fact that we didn't have reporters and statisticians following us from game to game to keep track of the players' performance and statistics. Unfortunately, a lot of that history was lost. The press always covered Sunday league games, but a majority of the games that were played throughout the week in small towns throughout the country went virtually unnoticed by the press. There were players posting incredible feats in those games, but the records have all been lost with time.

With the onslaught of integration in the great American pastime, the East coast teams had taken a much bigger hit than the Midwest teams. In time, they began to throw in the towel one by one. As the Negro National League folded, the Negro American League had to take action in order to maintain a championship series each season. So the league divided itself into two divisions—the East and West—with five teams in each. The Eastern Division teams included the Baltimore Elite Giants, the Indianapolis Clowns, the New York Cubans, the Philadelphia Stars, and the Louisville Buckeyes. My chief duties gave me complete jurisdiction over the umpiring crews for the Western Division, which consisted of the Memphis Red Sox, the Chicago American Giants, the Houston Eagles (formerly of Newark), the Birmingham Black Barons, and the ever-faithful Monarchs of Kansas City.

During our meeting, Martin also asked me a series of questions about my family background, education, umpiring experience, other job experiences, military service, and goals for the future. Not wanting to upset the apple cart after just getting hired, I mentioned nothing of my aspirations to make it to the majors. But Martin must have read my mind because *he* brought it up. "Young man," he started, "what about the majors? Shouldn't that be a goal for you? Not that I would want to lose another talented young man to those vultures, but you should make that a goal for yourself. It is within reach, you know."

I was completely caught off guard by his suggestion. Here was someone who verbalized the dream that I had held, but ever since Jackie Robinson's signing kept to myself. Surely the majors must be attainable if someone of Martin's stature said so. I was reeling from the rush of excitement as he told me about the different umpiring schools around the country that I should investigate. There, I could learn more about the proper techniques of umpiring. *A school for umpires?* I thought to myself. *What can they teach me that I don't already know?* I quickly brought myself back down to earth after realizing that surely if there are schools for umpiring, then there must be a lot more I could learn about the job.

Before he sent me on my way, Martin handed me an article he had torn out of an old issue of *Reader's Digest* entitled, "The Ten Commandments of Umpiring." He advised me as he shook my hand goodbye: "Young man, if you can abide by these rules, and the Lord's Ten Commandments, then you'll be all right." Barely glancing at the article, I tucked it into my pants pocket and headed out the door with a world of possibilities swirling through my head.

Once back in my hotel room, I took out the article and read it. Written by the president of Major League Baseball's National League, Ford Frick, the commandments of umpiring were a series of suggestions that served as a motivational tool, one that I would continue to refer to often during the years that I umpired. As a matter of fact, I carried that piece of paper with me to every game I umpired for years, well into the 1960s. Unfortunately, that original article has long since met its fate, but it faithfully lasted me over 15 years. To this day, those commandments are engrained in my mind.

Although I admit that I didn't always adhere to each mandate, I did try to respect them as if they were of divine inspiration. Each of them made a lot of sense to me, and apparently to many other umpires as well, as today you can still find them posted in plenty of umpires' dressing rooms in both minor and major league parks.

Here are The Ten Commandments of Umpiring, along with a few comments from me:

- *Keep your eye on the ball.* I always did, especially when Satchel Paige was on the mound.
- *Keep all personalities out of your work. Forget and forgive.* A useful tip, but for the life of me, I don't know why this commandment does not apply to players and managers, too.
- *Avoid sarcasm. Don't insist on the last word.* Okay, at least I abided by half of this commandment, as I don't think I was ever sarcastic. There was never a need to be. But I always got in my favorite last three words when a situation got out of hand: "You're outta here!"
- *Never charge a player, and above all no pointing your finger and yelling.* Again, shouldn't this commandment apply for players and managers, instead of umpires?
- *Hear only the things you should hear; be deaf to others.* I admit, this is another commandment that I didn't always take to heart. I am by nature a nosey person, so I always listened to what was going on around me.
- *Keep your temper. A decision made in anger is never sound.* I pat myself on the back because my decisions were always made in the context of authority, not anger.
- *Watch your language.* I can also say that I never cursed a player or manager—although it was hard to resist in some instances.
- *Take pride in your work at all times. Remember, respect for an umpire is created off the field as well as on.* This was actually Commandment No. 1 for me. I always took great pride in every call I made.
- *Review your work. You will find, if you are honest, that 90 percent of the trouble is traceable to loafing.* Not to be braggadocios, but the one thing you won't hear someone say about me is that I was a lazy umpire.

• *No matter what your opinion of another umpire, never make an adverse comment regarding him. To do so is despicable and ungentlemanly.* Human nature makes it hard to resist this temptation. Still, I don't believe I talked poorly of my colleagues while I was an umpire.

WHEN I RETURNED TO KANSAS CITY from my meeting with Dr. J. B. Martin in Memphis, I was fired up. Immediately, I went right to work composing letters, sending out schedules, making suggestions for assignments, and calling my fellow umpires. It was a lot of busy work, but I enjoyed it immensely.

It turns out that I didn't have to work all that hard, however. On my first road assignment for an exhibition game in Little Rock, Arkansas, with the Monarchs, I discovered that my chiefly orders had fallen on deaf ears. Most of the umpires working under me had been at this a lot longer than I had, and they already had a fixed routine. One of the local umpires told me flatly, "You ain't got to be writing letters to umpires all over the country. Man, we know you coming before you do."

The reason was simple: when it came to promoting a game, no one did it better than the Negro Leagues. Window placards, newspaper advertisements, sound trucks with blaring loudspeakers mounted atop them, and word of mouth were in the works well in advance of most games. Umpires knew from that information, as well as being in contact with local team owners and business managers, to have their crews ready for action. That was fine by me because it made my job that much easier.

Whenever I checked in with Martin I never let him in on the secret of the age-old system of Negro League umpires. All he knew is that I was one of his most efficient and effective chief umpires, and I always had my fellow umpires under control. That was just the way he—and I—liked it.

6

THE GREAT
SATCHEL PAIGE

"Satchel had no peers, no fears, because he was the best!
You hit him once, you don't hit him too many more times;
that's just the way it was!"

* Marvin Price, Chicago American Giants *

TO BORROW A LINE FROM SATCHEL himself, "Ain't no maybe so about it:" Satchel Paige was absolutely *the best* pitcher I ever saw or umpired, hands down. Sure there were other standouts in the leagues like Hilton Smith, Joe Black, Andy Porter, and Wilmer Fields who could keep pace. But no one was more unpredictable or masterful than the fabled Leroy "Satchel" Paige. Satchel was *the* perennial Negro Leagues All-Star. A formidable presence on the mound, his unmatched style and personality made him not only the biggest box-office draw in the history of the league, but also its most recognizable and beloved figure.

I first saw Satchel pitch upon my arrival in Kansas City during the 1946 season. I had heard about him as a child when Locker

Burns spoke of having seen him barnstorm through Birmingham, Alabama. His name was legendary when I lived in Dayton. Even while firing off rounds in Okinawa, black soldiers from every part of the country reminisced about having seen the great Satchel Paige. In Kansas City, he was godlike. Even now, some 60 years after first laying eyes on him in person, I can tell you from my personal experience, everything you have heard or read about the magnitude of his talent is not an exaggeration. Words cannot do justice to his prowess. But I'll try anyway: Satchel Paige was simply a phenom!

By the time I came onto the scene as an umpire, Satchel was 40 years old, but his stuff was still incredible at that age. I can't even begin to imagine what he must have been like in his prime. It's unthinkable. He threw with astonishing precision and power. Wherever he wanted the ball to go, it went. I can confidently say in all the innings I umpired Satchel, I never saw him make a ham-handed pitch. Even when he didn't throw a strike, it was always just barely off either corner of the plate—but *never* far out of the strike zone. Sometimes it seemed as if he'd purposely throw with a little less zip on the ball, aiming it a tad too high, low, inside, or wide of his target, as if teasing the batter, giving him a false sense of hope that maybe, just maybe, he could make contact with that ball. Then Satchel would let loose a blistering pitch that would strut across the plate so fast I'd swear a cool breeze was a-blowing as the ball popped into the catcher's mitt. The man could simply bring it!

Nothing compares to the sound of an oncoming Satchel fastball. The moment he released the ball from his hand, it sounded as if a swarm of killer bees was coming down the pike, humming all the way. With most pitchers, a batter can begin to hear the oncoming pitch when it gets about halfway to the plate, and in some cases a little earlier if they are throwing some good heat; but with Satchel it was upon release. He threw smoke. I kid you not, if a hitter blinked his eyes while Satchel was in his delivery, then there was no way in hell he was going to be able to pick the ball back up again. He might as well just stand there and wait for my strike call. (And many batters did.) On occasion, hitters struggled so mightily to catch up to his heater that they had yet to finish their swing as the catcher was preparing to throw the ball back to the mound.

Hitters were baffled, if not terrified, by Satchel's pitches. After striking out, most guys simply laughed and shook their heads in disbelief, shrugging off their poor at-bat almost as if being mowed down by the great one was a badge of honor. Satchel made a lot of the best hitters look like they should have been playing in a tee-ball league. Some of those poor guys looked so pathetic that I had to keep myself from laughing out loud. Even the oh-so-powerful Willie Mays had trouble with Paige. After surrendering a double to Mays the first time he faced him, Satchel told Mays his next time up, "That's it, kid." As Mays put it, "The next three times I came up to bat it was *whoosh, whoosh, whoosh!*"

I've seen many a pitcher get creamed during a game, but batters never beat up on Satchel. As a matter of fact, I can't recall ever seeing anyone hit a home run off him. A few guys like Goose Curry and Sherwood Brewer knocked him around pretty good, but hitters who made solid contact off Satchel were few and far between. He came right after the hitter, rarely walking a batter—and never intentionally.

By the time I started umpiring, Satchel only pitched the first three innings of a game, and then he was done. He was the biggest name in the league: his name alone assured owners and promoters of sell-out crowds. He pitched often, but only for those nine (usually quick) outs. Most typically, "Satchel's caddies" were workhorse relievers like Hall of Famer Hilton Smith and hard-throwing right-hander Booker McDaniel. Smith, who was as close to perfection as you could get this side of Satchel, would come on after Paige's three innings were up. He was just as effective as Satchel, except he didn't have the showmanship or personality. On the mound, Satchel entertained the fans—a showman, *yes*; a showoff, *no*. He was cocky, self-assured, and conceited, which was fine by me, because at least he had the stuff to back it up. He was just a hell of a pitcher and he knew it.

In my career, I had to throw quite a few pitchers out of games for cursing me and questioning my calls. But I never threw Satchel out, although I did come close one particular game at Blues Stadium. Satchel had thrown one of his nasty drop pitches, and it barely missed the inside part of the plate. Satchel thought everything he threw was a strike, and most times he was right—but not this time. Unhappy with my call, he walked halfway toward home plate and glared at me like he wanted to rip my eyes out. Not one to be intimidated, I yanked off my facemask, walked around in front of the catcher, and shot my meanest Dick Tracy-esque stare right back at him.

Satchel snapped, "Did you miss one, ump?"

I snapped right back, "Naw, I didn't miss nothing."

Our intense stare down continued a few seconds more until Satchel whisked around and went back to the mound, as if to say, "Okay you blind bastard, I'll show you!" Satchel hurled a blistering fastball that made a beeline down the heart of the plate for a called strike three, then looked at me as if to say, *Uh-huh, I thought so. Ain't no maybe so about it!*

My first time calling balls and strikes for Satchel, I wasn't as nervous as I was anxious before the game. I had seen him pitch a dozen times or so from the stands and while umpiring the bases, but being behind the plate was a whole new ballgame. I considered calling balls and strikes for the master to be a true test of my ability.

As the umpires took the field, Frank Duncan hollered at me in a most mischievous tone, "Kid, this is Satchel. Keep your eye on the ball!" As Satchel's first pitch came sailing toward the catcher's mitt, I began to appreciate Duncan's message. The pitch zigzagged across the plate in a way I had never seen a baseball move. It all happened so fast; I was stunned, and so was the batter. For a split second I was caught off guard, then realized I had yet to make the call. I bellowed, *"S-T-T-T-R-R-R-I-I-I-K-E,"* proudly calling my first Satchel Paige pitch.

As the first inning progressed with Satchel continuing to hurl heat at batters, I noticed that his pitches seemed to pick up more speed *and* movement. I again thought back to Duncan's comment and the first rule of the Ten Commandments of Umpiring: "Keep your eye on the ball." The pitches were so dodgy that I thought Duncan must have meant that Satchel might be throwing some *tricky* balls. I thought to myself, *He must be doctoring the ball, because what I'm seeing ain't humanly possible.* Thinking I was on top of my game, I called time to check a thrown ball for cuts or nicks. The sucker was clean as a whistle.

In the second inning his pitches were dipping and darting even more. It seemed Satchel was just now getting loose. The movement on each pitch was inconceivable, so again I checked the ball to see if it had been tampered with—and found it clean. A couple batters later, I checked the ball yet again, this time looking down the third-base line at Duncan, who was obviously tickled by the naiveté of this young ump. I then glanced back at Satchel, who upon catching my eye quipped, "Hey, rook, you ain't use to ol' Satch yet. But you will be." From then on I never checked another ball thrown by Satchel Paige.

Satchel was very crafty and clever when it came to the art of pitching. As a batter, the trick to keeping up with him was not to take your eyes off his pitching hand during his wind up and delivery. He knew how to deceive batters with body motion alone. In his wind up, he would try to confuse the hitter by the movements of his long, lanky frame and his size-14 shoes. Some batters figured this out, but most were just screwed.

But deception wasn't Satchel's only weapon. He also had a full repertoire of pitches, each of which had different movements. In addition to his fast and curveballs, he had other "specialty pitches" that were just as deadly, including: the 4-Day-Rider, the Ally-oops, the Bat Dodger, the Step 'n' Pitch It, the Midnight Creeper, the Drop Ball, the Jump Ball, the Wobbly Ball, and the Be Ball (named so because he said the pitch would "be's where I throws it"). But none was more wicked than his infamous hesitation pitch, in which he would kick his long, thin leg sky high, twist around toward second base, wind back around toward home plate, plant his foot, pump his arm, hesitate … and then hurl! Batters had a tough time getting around on it because, like his body motion, the ball was off speed—seeming to slow up, and then take off. After he made it to the majors, the hesitation pitch—or more appropriately his delivery—was outlawed. The rulebook states that once a pitcher starts his wind up he cannot stop his motion toward the plate. The rule wasn't made specifically for Satchel Paige's unhittable hesitation pitch, but it sure did take one of his best pitches out of his arsenal.

There were no radar guns in those days, but even into his 40s, Satchel was likely throwing around 100 miles per hour. There's no doubt in my mind. The only starting pitcher I would possibly compare him to today would be Randy Johnson in his prime, but that's being generous to Johnson. Johnson's physique and form are very similar to Paige's, but even as overpowering as he is, Johnson is missing some of the zip and accuracy.

Because gloves were not as high quality in those days, catchers in the Negro Leagues used all types of items to pad the inside of their mitts as protection. Otherwise, a catcher's hand would get eaten up by the ball. Sponges, raw meat, rags, and newspapers were some of the more common objects that helped soften the blow of oncoming pitches. That worked some of the time, but not when Satchel was on the mound. I felt sorry for Monarchs catchers Elston Howard and Earl Taborn, as they winced each time one of Satchel's stinging fastballs landed in their glove. Satchel threw so hard that many times the catcher literally fell back into me due to the force of the pitch.

Negro League catching and pitching star Ted "Double Duty" Radcliffe, who I got to know later in life, had the gnarliest, ugliest, most deformed fingers I have ever seen. His catching hand had been bent and battered from—as he said—"catching Satchel's heat for over 20 years." Duty once told me, "Catching Satchel is like trying to catch a freight train barreling at you with the brakes gone bad!" And from what I saw, he was hardly exaggerating.

The "brush back" pitch was common in the Negro Leagues. Not only did many pitchers brush 'em back, they'd knock 'em down if necessary. I saw quite a few guys get cold cocked (and this was in the days before the batting helmet). It was nothing to hear a manager yell from the dugout, "Knock his head off!" There was nothing in the rulebook that stated it was illegal, so it was fair game. Unlike in today's baseball, I never once had a fight break out over a pitcher brushing someone back; it was all part of aggressive Negro baseball. As a matter of fact, many times after games I'd overhear opponents teasing each other about how they had to duck and dodge pitches trying to get out of harm's way. But unlike many of the league's best pitchers, Satchel never used such bullying tactics.

He may not have been book smart, but Satchel knew how to use psychology to mess with the hitter. He was legendary for calling his outfielders in to the infield and having his entire defense lounge around the infield as he'd mow down batter after batter. I had heard about this tactic for years and finally bore witness to it for the first time at a game in Indianapolis. In the second inning, Satchel beckoned for me to come toward the mound. "Hey ump," he said to me, "these guys ain't no match for Satchel. I'm gonna get 'em all out. I'm calling in my players." Astonished, I regained my composure and replied, "Satch, that's fine. But you know the rules state you must have nine men on the playing field at all times, otherwise your pitch doesn't count." I continued, "You can call them in, but they must remain inside the white lines in fair territory." Obviously well aware of the rules after having done this numerous times, Satchel turned around and motioned his players in. As his teammates sat around the infield as if they were at a Sunday picnic in the park, Satchel threw *nine straight jacks*, and, as easy as counting from one to three, struck out the side!

When he wasn't having his way with opposing hitters or putting on a show for the fans, Satchel was quite a poet in his own right. Much like baseball legend Yogi Berra, he possessed incredible wit and wisdom. Some of his more infamous quips or "Satchisms" are: "You have to believe in yourself. When you believe, you do."; "Avoid fried meats which angry up the blood."; "Ain't no man can avoid being average, but ain't no man got to be common."; "Age is a question of mind over matter. If you don't mind, it don't matter."; "Don't look back—something might be gaining on you."; "My pitching philosophy is simple: keep the ball away from the bat."; "Don't pray when it rains if you don't pray when the sun shines."; "Too many pitchers got the hurry-ups. Slow down, you last longer."; "Throw strikes. Home plate don't move."; "If you can't overpower 'em, outcute 'em."; and "We don't stop playing because we get old. We get old because we stop playing."

In my early twenties trying to look citified after moving from small-town Alabama to small-city Ohio.

Relaxing during chow time while serving in Japan during World War II.

In my Marine uniform. All that's missing is the Purple Heart I was awarded.

ABOVE: Opening Day at Blues Stadium in Kansas City in 1949 as the Monarchs hosted the Philadelphia Stars. From left to right: KC manager Buck O'Neil, Sylvester Vaughn, me, Frank Duncan, and Stars manager Oscar Charleston.

BELOW: Barnstorming wasn't easy. Standing alongside the road with the Monarchs after our team bus burned to a crisp in Florida.

ABOVE and BELOW: Promotional photos taken in 1950 showcase my signature style that I developed in the Negro Leagues. The photos may not be "real," but that's exactly how I umpired during games.

ABOVE: Proof positive that I am who I say I am—my umpire card from the 1950 season, signed by Negro American League president Dr. J. B. Martin.

BELOW: Al Somers Umpire School was much harder than it looks in this photo of me practicing my "safe" call.

December 13, 1956

Mr. Robert Motley
1600 West 37th Street
Kansas City, Missouri

Your letter, application and check for $20.00 received and this letter will serve as a receipt for the $20.00.

We are going to have a fine class as we have about fifteen boys coming back for the advance course from last year. Most of these boys were placed in Minor League jobs last season. So far, we have four Negro boys signed and I do expect several more. I am sure that you will enjoy our school very much and our methods of teaching.

I just returned from the Minor League Convention which was held in Jacksonville, Florida, while attending the meetings, I placed about 35 boys in higher classification of jobs. I had several meetings with the American and National Leagues also the National Association, in reference to conducting a National Umpire School next year.

Will close now with my very best wishes to you and will be looking forward to meeting you on January 18th. Happy Holliday Greetings.

Sincerely,

Al Somers

Al Somers

After seven long years of waiting, I was finally allowed into umpire school in 1957. Here's the letter Al Somers sent to notify me.

ABOVE: The top graduates of the class of 1957 at Al Somers Umpire School. From left to right: Richard DeChaine, Harold Wymers, Al Somers, Al Salerno, and me.

BELOW: Umpire school buddies in 1958. From left to right: Henry Johnson; Carlos Sanchez; Lou DiMuro (kneeling), who became a major league umpire; me with my daughter, Bobette; and Grover Carr.

Painting the town with my wife, Pearline, soon after our marriage in 1952.

Clowning at home with my daughter, Bobette, in 1956.

My son Byron and me in 1960.

ABOVE: My Pacific Coast League debut on August 18, 1958 was newsworthy.

BELOW LEFT: At Kauffman Stadium in the mid-1990s with filmmaker Ken Burns (center) and Buck O'Neil (right). Burns threw out the first pitch to Buck, and I called the pitch a strike.

BELOW RIGHT: Standing in front of my display case at the Negro League Baseball Museum in Kansas City, Missouri.

Satchel was particularly aware of that last one. That's why he pitched for so long.

HALFWAY THROUGH THE 1948 SEASON, Satchel was signed by the Cleveland Indians, which made him the oldest rookie in Major League Baseball history at the age of 42. Some thought Satchel's signing was a publicity stunt by the Indians' eccentric owner, Bill Veeck. But Satchel silenced his critics after finishing his first half-season in the majors with six victories, only one loss, and a 2.48 ERA. He also made history by becoming the first black man to ever pitch in a World Series as the Indians defeated the Boston Braves that year.

Once he left the Negro Leagues, I thought I'd never have another opportunity to umpire one of his games. But sure enough, in 1950, after two short seasons in the majors, Satchel came home to the Negro Leagues and continued pitching to thrilled crowds nationwide. He bounced back to the majors in 1951, joining the St. Louis Browns for a few seasons; but he later returned to his roots in the Negro Leagues when he was in his late 40s. He continued to pitch even when most of his opponents on the mound were half his age.

In September 1965, Satchel pitched his last professional outing. Charlie O. Finley, owner of the Kansas City Athletics, was as wildly innovative in running a baseball team as Satchel was delivering a hesitation pitch. Finley invited the legend to join the A's and pitch three innings of a game, in order for Satchel to qualify to receive a well-deserved major league pension. I took my family to see him throw that day. The 58-year-old was on top of his game, stunning the crowd by pitching three shutout innings against a powerful Boston Red Sox lineup. The only batter to get a hit off him was future Hall of Famer Carl Yastrzemski.

Satchel was full of life, downright silly at times. Sometimes he was so animated on the ball diamond, I found myself laughing at his conversations even though I wasn't even a part of them. His toothy smile and his dry, throaty, sinister laughter were his trademarks. However, he could be brooding, moody, even out-and-out mean at times. I saw him snap at umpires—myself included—and his teammates. If one of his teammates flubbed a routine play, Satchel would shoot him a look that could kill. Between innings I would see Satchel yank that player into the runway of the dugout—out of sight of the crowd—and rip into him. On bus rides, his teammates would occasionally talk about his moodiness and his high expectations. No one ever talked bad about Satchel, though. They were always respectful and awed by his stature, but were well aware of his intolerance for mediocrity.

His teammates could talk about him on the bus because Satchel never rode the bus—at least not during the times when I traveled with the Monarchs. Either he or his valet—a tall, slender, nerdy, dark-skinned man everybody called "Jew Baby"—would drive Satchel's Cadillac from town to town. After all, he was a superstar. That was just his style. I wouldn't say Satchel was a classy guy, but he was definitely stylish. His clothes were fashionable and he always walked with the confident swagger of a movie star, both on and off the field. It was nothing to see him drive up to a stadium in a brand-spanking-new Cadillac every couple months.

When you're at the level of a Satchel Paige, you're pretty much invincible and can do whatever you please, which was especially true in those days. Whatever demands he made of owners and booking agents, they were happy to oblige, and deservedly so. He demanded a percentage of the box-office receipts and top dollar—which he got. He answered to no one. Buck O'Neil, manager of the Monarchs during part of Satchel's reign, was once quoted as saying, "You don't manage Satchel Paige. You manage the team he happens to be on."

Even his manager with the St. Louis Browns, Marty Marion, noted, "He ran the club, not me!"

Most games Satchel arrived whenever he felt like it, apparently living by his own motto: "I never rush myself. They can't start the game without me." Sometimes he'd arrive an hour early; other times, for a 12 o'clock start he might stroll in at 11:59, just to make everyone fidgety about whether he would show or not. He sure didn't need any preparation. In all the years that I umpired him, I never once saw Satch warm up in the bullpen before a game. He'd lope out to the mound, take a few moments to look around at the crowd as if acknowledging his legions of worshipers, toss four or five easy pitches to his catcher, and then it was on. He'd rear back and start firing. The man simply had it in him.

Years after we had both retired from baseball, I would run into Satchel at various events around Kansas City. We were always courteous with one another, although we never held a conversation other than a friendly greeting. As a matter of fact, I've often wondered if he ever even knew my name. But, he would always nod, smile ever so slightly, and say, "How ya doing, ump?" To be honest, I don't care if he ever knew my name or not, it was just an honor to be recognized by the greatest pitcher of all-time, Leroy "Satchel" Paige.

7

AN EYEWITNESS
TO GREATNESS

"Playing in the Negro Leagues was probably one of
the most rewarding experiences I ever had in my life.
I can never forget it."

* Hank Aaron *

THROUGH THE YEARS, I'VE HEARD numerous baseball
historians and former players declare that the "real" Negro Leagues
ended when Jackie Robinson entered Major League Baseball in 1947.
They claim that the black leagues were so decimated by the majors
taking their best ballplayers, that the level of play in the Negro
Leagues became "second-rate." With all due respect, these folks
obviously did not observe the phenomenal players that I was
eyewitness to on a daily basis. They didn't *see* what I saw. I know my
baseball and can tell you first-hand, many of the guys I umpired in
the late 1940s through the mid-1950s could have been big-league
athletes—if given the chance.

True, many of the East coast teams were financially devastated by
Jackie's entrance, because they had to compete against the major

league box office. Black fans preferred to go see one of their own playing in the big leagues rather than go to a Negro League game. But in the Midwest and South, black baseball continued to thrive for several years following the black players' great migration into the majors.

It's more accurate to say that at this juncture the Negro Leagues became a "breeding ground" for the majors. Once the majors got a whiff of a good ballplayer he was quickly scooped up. That potential to get spotted by a scout from the big leagues only further encouraged Negro Leaguers to put forth their best effort in every game. That raised the level of competition and kept the league vital, so I take issue when someone says the "real" Negro Leagues ended in 1947. Try telling that to guys like Hank Aaron, Willie Mays, Ernie Banks, or Elston Howard. A league that spawns those players—let alone others like Sam Jethroe, Joe Black, Al Smith, or "Sweet Lou" Johnson—is anything but second rate.

There are quite a few celebrated major league ballplayers who got their start in the Negro Leagues. I had the privilege of umpiring three in particular—Aaron, Banks, and Mays—long before they became the Hall of Fame legends they are today. All three in my estimation were standouts even as Negro League rookies. The world found out about their greatness once they joined the majors, but I can proudly say that I predicted early on that each would go on to have illustrious big-league careers.

Oftentimes my umpire buddy Mark Van Buren and I would talk about the potential of different players we saw on a regular basis. To pass the time, we developed a rating game we called, "Who's any good?" There were times when we might go weeks without seeing each other, but when we were together again we'd compare notes and ask each other if we had seen anybody new of note. That's how the game got its start. We usually played this game with the rookies. We had three levels of ratings: "Shiner" was highest; "Scootch" in the middle; and "Scab" the lowest. We'd also give "pluses" and "minuses" if we thought a guy was borderline. We were tough judges and reserved the "Shiner" level only for those we thought for sure could break into the majors. Years later I enjoyed teaching and playing the game with my son.

I pegged Aaron, Banks, Mays, and a few others as "Shiner pluses" from the get go. Their potential was that obvious. Of the three, Van Buren thought only Banks was of "Shiner-plus" quality, although I recall he eventually gave Aaron a "Scootch triple-plus" rating. When Van Buren and I would run into each other years later—after all these guys we had rated were established All-Stars or big-time flops—I would always tease him, "Well, VB, I hate to say I told you so, but . . ." All he could do was grimace and laugh.

Even in the infancy of their careers, Aaron, Banks, and Mays each carried themselves like they were something special. They were not cocky, but definitely confident—born with an innate awareness that they possess a special gift that makes them a cut above the rest. I found myself paying closer attention to these guys just because of the way they handled themselves. That "star quality" drew my eyes to their every move, both on and off the field.

HANK AARON HAD NOT DEVELOPED into the power hitter he would later become when he first joined the Indianapolis Clowns in 1952, although he did belt a few homers. What impressed me most was that this lanky kid was consistent in making contact with the ball. He would almost slap at the ball, probably because he had not yet developed the correct grip on the bat. Oddly enough, he batted cross-handed. Instead of his right hand being on top of his left, which is standard for a right-handed hitter, he had it reversed. I probably would have never even noticed his peculiar grip had it not been for the Clowns' loud and boisterous manager, Buster Haywood. Aaron's grip used to drive Haywood nuts.

During pregame batting practice, I'd occasionally observe Haywood and some of the other Clowns players working with Aaron, trying to get him to undo his unusual batting habit. But every time Aaron stepped up to the plate, he'd revert back to his comfort level—much to his manager's disgust. Haywood was always high-strung and animated during games. He would try in vain to contain himself, sitting reclined on the team bench, observing the action like an overseer keeping tabs on his field hands. But then the slightest little thing would set him off. On a few occasions when I was behind the plate, I heard him get after Aaron. The future home run king would step in the batter's box and take his stance, and Haywood would leap up from his seat as if he had just been goosed, and dart to the top of the dugout stairs. "Boy, uncross them damn hands," Haywood would yell at the top of his lungs. "I done told you about that!" Once Aaron started smacking extra-base hits, however, Haywood learned to keep his mouth shut.

Aaron was a skinny, dark-skinned, slightly awkward looking young man. He was just a kid, but he had an obvious God-given gift to play the game of baseball. During his early days in the Negro Leagues, he was a shortstop. He could move easily from side to side and was a decent fielder. But he was there for his hitting: during his brief stint in the Negro Leagues he regularly pounded a battery of some of the world's toughest pitchers to the tune of an average well above .400.

I'm one of the few who can lay claim to being there when Aaron began his illustrious journey into the baseball record books, as I just happened to have been assigned to travel with the Indianapolis Clowns on a barnstorming tour through the South in 1951. It was while the Clowns were playing an exhibition game in Aaron's hometown of Mobile, Alabama, that the kid was first noticed by

Haywood. The Clowns took on an all-black semi-pro team, the Mobile Black Bears, for which Aaron played. The Black Bears won the contest, and Aaron performed well enough to impress Haywood.

I would have paid little attention to Aaron, The Black Bears, or Mobile had it not been for the always animated Haywood. Once we boarded the bus to head off to the next town, Haywood was on fire about "that boy Aaron." Pacing up and down the aisle, he finally settled into a seat a couple rows in front of me. Sounding like a broken record, Haywood began discussing Aaron with the team's business manager, whose name I've long forgotten. Haywood, a Southerner himself, had a thick drawl and often had a hard time properly enunciating certain words. The more sophisticated the word, the more he'd butcher the pronunciation. Over and over Haywood kept telling the business manager, "Believe you me, that boy Aaron, he got 'potenchical.'" Finally after hearing him slaughter the word "potential" one too many times, Sherwood Brewer, one of the team's infielders, butted in: "Coach! The word is po-ten-tial!" Haywood snapped back, "That's what I said nigga, potenchical!" I had to bury my face in my breast protector to keep from laughing out loud.

Sure enough, that next season, Haywood got his wish: Hank Aaron became a member of the Indianapolis Clowns. Haywood's euphoria over his recruiting conquest was short-lived, however, when halfway through the 1952 season Aaron found himself on his way to the minor leagues to play with the Eau Claire Bears of the Northern League. After finally developing the correct hold on the bat, Aaron tore up the minor leagues. By 1954 he had joined the Milwaukee Braves, and, as we all know, the rest is baseball history.

NEGRO LEAGUE PLAYERS DID whatever they could to get an edge. When it came to pitching, almost anything was fair game in the Negro Leagues. Pitchers were notorious for throwing all types of illegal pitches, and I saw them all: spit balls, shine balls, emory balls, and some that probably never even had names. They danced so wickedly on their way to the plate that even a blind man would know the balls had been doctored.

Pitchers' tactics were varied. Some purposely slicked their hair down with the popular hair grease Sweet Georgia Brown. They would run their hands across the top of their head (pretending they were wiping off sweat) to lube up their hand and then the ball. But I was well aware of all the tricks of the trade, and if I saw a pitcher going to his brow too often or into his pocket too much, then that was a telltale sign that he was up to something. I caught pitchers with all kinds of ball-altering items in their pockets: razors, knives, nail files, screwdrivers, needles, even sand. You name it, they would try it—anything they could smuggle onto the field to rough up the ball and make it jitterbug across the plate.

But not everyone needed to doctor the ball to be successful. One pitcher who was amongst the best I ever saw—and who didn't rely on trick pitches—was Baltimore Elite Giants right-handed hurler Joe Black. On the mound and in life Joe Black was no joke—he was the real deal. Big and burly, Black was 6-foot-2 and 210 pounds of pure power. He had been in the Negro Leagues for several seasons before finally advancing to the majors at the age of 28 in 1952 with the Brooklyn Dodgers, where he earned the National League Rookie of the Year award after going 15-4 with a 2.15 ERA. He also became the first black pitcher in the history of the majors to win a World Series game later that same season. Black only played about six seasons in the big leagues. It's too bad that he, like so many other well-aged Negro League stars, didn't have a chance to shine on the big stage in the early prime of his career. But while in the Negro Leagues he was as good as it got.

Black was truly an overpowering hurler with an insane fastball. Even the best hitters had a tough time getting around on it. Lester Lockett once fouled off so many of Black's fastballs in an at-bat that the crowd grew restless—as did I. After having over a dozen of his fastballs foul-tipped by the right-handed-hitting Lockett, Black fired off the nastiest slider I've ever seen. The ball looked like it was going to pelt Lockett in his ribs, but at the last second it shot back across the heart of the plate, belt high. It shocked the heck out of me! Excited by the beautiful pitch, my instincts sent me flying into the air as I belted out, *"S-T-T-R-R-R-I-I-I-I-K-E T-H-H-R-R-E-E-E-E! YOU'RE OUT!"* Frozen and stunned, all Lockett could do was stand there looking like road kill after rigor mortis had set in.

Like the majority of the East Coast players, Joe Black was dignified and gentlemanly. I don't know why it was exactly, but the majority of East Coast players seemed to have a certain class about them. Whether they were more educated, I don't know, but they certainly carried themselves as if they were. Not to slight any of the other Negro players, but the Midwest and Southern teams seemed like they just picked up any old guy from a farming community as long as he could hit or pitch. Midwest and Southern players were more gruff and tough. Guys from the East like Roy Campanella, Elston Howard, Wilmer Fields, Junior Gilliam, Bob Scott, Mahlon Duckett, Stanley Glenn, Max Manning, and Bill "Ready" Cash seemed to be cut from a different cloth in the way they walked, talked, and dressed.

When Joe Black stepped on the mound, however, all the gracious behavior went out the window. He meant business. Looking dead serious and moving with an almost Marine-like bearing, he bullied batters into submission. He was a smart pitcher, knowing exactly where to put the pitch over the plate in order to play to a hitter's weakness. Black wasn't as whimsical as Satchel Paige or as silky smooth as Hilton Smith, but he had his own style on the mound: he just reared back and threw wickedly hard, like a prizefighter going for the knockout punch on every pitch.

Black was a tough old bird who didn't take shit from anybody. If he liked you, he loved you. If he didn't give a hoot for you, you knew that, too. Even when I reconnected with him in the mid-1990s before his death in 2002, he still had that "take no bullshit" attitude that I had grown accustomed to nearly 50 years earlier. Black put that attitude to work for him in helping out *all* his former Negro League brothers—even this last living umpire. For decades, he worked behind the scenes, fighting for monetary compensation for every individual who could prove an involvement in the Negro Leagues. Considering that he was already receiving a pension from Major League Baseball, Black could have relaxed and enjoyed his life, choosing not to be concerned with the livelihood of any of his fellow Negro League alums. But that just wasn't Joe Black. While many ignored and downplayed my contributions as a "former Negro Leaguer" because I wasn't a player, Black always fought on my behalf, stating, "Bob Motley was an umpire in our league, and he should get every bit of recognition and pension like the rest of us." For that fight on my behalf, and for all of his lobbying efforts on behalf of *every* living Negro Leaguer, and for the memories I cherish of his masterful wizardry on the mound, I will always hold a deep admiration and respect for the man.

Incidentally, despite the efforts of Joe and others, while many former Negro League players, who put in less time in the leagues than I did, have been awarded pensions, I have never earned one single dime in reparation from Major League Baseball or the World Umpires Association.

EVERY TIME I THINK ABOUT the lightning speed and the agile fielding of Ernie Banks I get goose bumps. What an athlete! For the modern-day comparison, he had the effortless grace of a Derek

Jeter, a guy who can make the toughest play look like a walk in the park. And also like Jeter, Banks was an all-around dynamo on the diamond; it didn't surprise me one bit when after being signed by the Chicago Cubs he bypassed the minors and went straight to the majors.

Banks was as tough a competitor as there ever was. He, like all the other black ballplayers of the time who made it to the majors, had to be. He couldn't be "just as good" as his white counterparts. He had to be better than they were just to make the squad; and then he had to maintain a certain level and attitude to stay. Banks proved his competitive edge by taking the high road—keeping his mouth shut and letting his bat do the talking. After being brushed back and knocked down by some pretty reputable pitchers, Banks would get right back in the batter's box and try to knock the very next pitch out of the park.

He became an immediate crowd favorite with Chicago fans. Donned "Mr. Cub," he played his entire 19-year career with the Cubs franchise. The love that major league fans showed him didn't surprise me, as his friendly demeanor, quick hands and glove, and big bat had also made him one of the darlings of the 1950 Kansas City Monarchs team. As a rookie with the Monarchs, Banks had the finesse and polish of a much more seasoned athlete. His glove was like a vacuum—not much got past him in the field. I used to hope that batters would hit a bullet in his direction just to watch him lunge, gather, spin, and fire to first. He used to spin around so fast; dust would swirl around him like he was caught up in a cyclone. He was something else!

A rock-solid hitter, too, Banks could drive the ball with power to every part of the field. But speed was a part of his game as well. I saw him collect his fair share of bunt singles, and if he was on third base, the pitcher was a nervous wreck as Banks danced off the bag, threatening to steal home.

In his first season with the Monarchs, Banks teamed up with another standout, veteran second baseman Gene Baker. Baker had been a whiz in the number-four position with the Monarchs since 1948, but when Banks came on the scene, the two brought out the best in each other. The double-play combination of Banks and Baker was the keystone for the Monarchs infield, and in my opinion has yet to be matched in the majors or anywhere else.

From what I observed of the two men, Banks and Baker couldn't have been more different from each other. Banks was more outgoing and had a vivacious personality. He always had a smile on his face and tons of youthful energy. On bus rides he would bound up and down the aisle, joshing with teammates, keeping them all entertained. Baker, on the other hand, was a lot more reserved and serious, seeming to conserve his energy for the game. I was impressed that he always had a book in his hand; apparently, he was educating himself, which was rare to see.

"Banks and Baker" became a catchphrase around Kansas City. You didn't talk about one without talking about the other. Strangely enough, Monarch fans would actually cheer for the opposing team to get a guy on first base, hoping to set up a Banks-Baker double-play situation. If a runner got on base, the whole stadium would be electrified, anticipating the lightning-fast acrobatic treat they had grown accustomed to from the duo.

In 1954, Baker joined Banks with the Cubs, making the pair the first black second base/shortstop combination in baseball history. I was shocked that the duo didn't take the majors by storm, and surprised and disappointed that Baker's career didn't evolve to superstar status the way Banks' had. I was certain that Baker too would have become a household name. Like Banks he was quite capable of knocking the daylight out of the ball, but his bat just couldn't light up major league pitching the way it did in the Negro Leagues. Baker was several years Banks' senior, so I'm sure that age must have played a big role in his performance.

Banks, on the other hand, was a whippersnapper, getting his first taste of the majors at age 22. He possessed sheer power and was destined for greatness from the word jump. He was a thrill to watch and a thrill to umpire, and it thrills me even today to be able to say, "Yep, I told you so!"

WILLIE MAYS WAS HANK AARON, Ernie Banks, and every other great player—black or white—rolled into one. It has been written that Mays is arguably the best baseball player in the history of the game, and he certainly gets my vote! He could do it all: hit, steal, catch, throw, and excite the crowd. These qualities were evident even in the early stages of his Negro League career. It was obvious to anyone who saw him that this young man was indeed a very unique and talented ballplayer.

Another product of the South, I got my first introduction to the talent of Willie Mays at Rickwood Field in Birmingham, Alabama, during his formative years as a member of the Birmingham Black Barons. Greatness has a way of calling attention to itself, and that was the case with Willie. He had the quick hands, the extra zip in his swing, the serious look on his face as he stepped up to the plate, the smooth glide in his stride as he sped across the base paths. There was also a hunger evident in how this youngster played the game.

During that game at Rickwood Field, the umpires from the Birmingham crew debated who was better, father or son, Willie Sr. or Willie Jr. In a game I umpired, Willie Mays' father—Willie Sr.—was playing center field for the Black Barons, while Willie Jr. was engaged at second base. It was very rare that a father and son were teammates, so it really gave people something to talk about.

Willie Sr. was outstanding, maybe even better than his son at that time—if you can imagine that. At the time, the father was probably in his 40s, but he impressed the hell out of me. I can only imagine how great he was when he was his son's age. He played the game the old-fashioned way—*hard*. Scrappy and cat-quick (hence his nickname, "Cat"), Willie Sr. was an "in your face" kind of player who would run right over you if you were in his way. Possessing a lot of nervous energy, Senior would pace around center field while waiting for the action. Once the ball was in the air, he'd take off as if he had been shot out of a cannon. It was easy to see where his son got his defensive skills from. Willie Sr. was sensational in the field; if a ball was hit anywhere in his vicinity, he was on it, sometimes even venturing out of his territory into left or right field to wave off his teammate and make a play.

This is no lie: I once saw Cat catch a ball one-handed behind his back, twirl around, and throw the ball on the fly to home plate in time to get a runner tagging from third. It sounds too good to be true, but I'm not exaggerating. Willie Sr., like his son, played for keeps.

The apple clearly didn't fall far from the tree. I got goose bumps watching Willie Jr.'s over-the-head basket catch in Game 1 of the 1954 World Series. I knew at that very moment that he was indeed a chip off the old block. Although Willie Jr. would eventually develop a style that was more fluid and polished than his father's, he never lost that feisty "in your face" quality he had inherited from the senior Mays. Since his father was born too soon to be considered for the majors, I was thrilled to see Junior take his father's brand of aggressive baseball—a hallmark of the Negro Leagues—to the bright lights of Major League Baseball.

THE ABSOLUTE BEST PLAYER I've ever seen in a baseball uniform—hands down—is Kansas City Monarchs centerfielder Willard Brown. Man, what a ballplayer! Brown was a spectacular player, what the scouts now call a "five-tool player," meaning that he could hit for power and average, run, field, and throw. I was thrilled when I learned that he had been selected to the Baseball Hall of Fame in 2006, as it was recognition that was long overdue.

Brown spent his entire career—except for a brief stint in the majors and the occasional stint in Latin America—with the Kansas City Monarchs. I got my first glimpse of him as a fan during the 1946 season. He was *the* standout on the team as far as I was concerned. I used to get a kick out of watching him mosey up to the plate like he could hardly walk. Talk about a decoy! When he hit that ball, he'd dash across those bases like a jackrabbit. He was the same way in the outfield. To look at him shuffle around like he was 99 years old, you'd think he was ready to collapse at any second. But let a ball come his way and he'd take off like a bullet. He was, in a word, thrilling.

I've heard a lot about the speed of Cool Papa Bell, who I unfortunately never got to see play, but even in his prime, I can't imagine Cool Papa being any faster than Willard Brown. I've also compared Brown to the likes of Willie Mays when Mays was at the top of his game. As great as we all know Mays was, in my opinion Brown was even better. Can you imagine that? What's even more astounding about the level of Brown's aptitude as a player is that I was seeing him toward the end of his career. Yet, even in his mid-to-late 30s he was making phenomenal plays in the outfield and beating that ball around the park. As with Satchel, I cannot even begin to wrap my mind around what ol' Brown must have been like in his prime.

In this day and age, athletes reap the benefits of state-of-the-art physical training, which allows them to stay healthier, age better, and play much longer. It's nothing to think of a Barry Bonds or a Randy Johnson playing into his 40s. But back in the day, unless you were Satchel, your career was most likely over at age 35. Forty tops!

Brown and Hank Thompson, also a member of the Monarchs' 1946 powerhouse team, became the third and fourth black players to make it to the majors within weeks after Jackie Robinson's historic debut and right on the heels of another Negro League great, Newark Eagles infielder Larry Doby. Jackie gets the most credit—and rightfully so because he was first. But Brown and Thompson made their own history by becoming the first two black players to appear in the same major league lineup for the St. Louis Browns.

Brown always hit well above .300 while in the Negro Leagues. However, in the few months he spent with the Browns, he wasn't nearly as productive. Maybe it was age (he was in his early 30s), maybe it was the competition level, maybe it was circumstances, or maybe it was being caught up in the pressure cooker of desegregation. Only Willard Brown could answer that question. But whatever the reason was, Brown couldn't quite cut it in the majors. His failure only further validates Jackie Robinson's awesome achievement—that despite the conditions around him Jackie was able to rise to the occasion during each of his ten major league seasons.

I first assumed it might have been Brown's age that had limited his output in the big leagues, but when he came back to the Monarchs in 1948 after the Browns didn't renew his contract, he continued tearing up Negro League pitching. So I'm inclined to think it was more of a comfort-level issue. Maybe in the majors, trying to be a pioneer, he just felt out of his element.

As great an athlete as he was, Brown always seemed to have a chip on his shoulder. I don't know if he was unhappy that he wasn't able to stick in the majors, or if he just had a moody personality, but he definitely carried the weight of some personal burden inside him. And although he never hassled me over a call nor showed any disrespect to any umpire, I just knew he was one fellow that I didn't want to cross.

An umpire is never supposed to have a favorite, but I must admit, as far as true talent and heart are concerned, Willard Brown was indeed mine.

IF BROWN WAS MY FAVORITE in the field, then my favorite in the dugout was manager Oscar Charleston. A Hall of Famer, Charleston was a big bruiser that I had seen play for the first time back in my younger years in Dayton. As a ballplayer Charleston had been as powerful a slugger as they come. From what I understand, he was second or third in terms of power to the great Josh Gibson. He was a Negro League legend, and I was honored to take the lineup card from his hand.

Like Buster Haywood, Charleston had managed two teams during his career, the Philadelphia Stars and the Indianapolis Clowns. As was true of most managers of the time, Buck O'Neil being one of the few exceptions, Charleston bounced around to whatever team needed him the most. Although he had an imposing physical presence at 6-foot-1 and 250 pounds, Charleston was a pussycat of a manager who treated both players and umpires with tremendous respect. He could have very easily been an intimidating force on the field—and maybe as a player he had been—but Charleston's demeanor was so calming you could have mistaken him for a man of the cloth as opposed to one of the top managers in baseball.

Unlike almost every other manager in the leagues, I never had one problem with Charleston. He was just a low-key kind of fellow who never raised his voice. If he did have a dispute about a call, he would simply walk up from the dugout and ask, almost in an apologetic tone, "What happened, ump?" Once I had explained the reason for my call he'd just nod or say, "Okay, ump," and go back to the dugout. He was the most calm and collected of gentlemen during some of the fiercest fought games, and I was always appreciative of his non-confrontational manner of managing.

I'VE SPOKEN ABOUT SEVERAL specific players, but in general the level of play on the whole was impressive in the Negro Leagues. These guys were tough competitors. They wanted nothing but to be the best and to play every day. The difference between today's game and the Negro Leagues only proves that. Pitchers today complain of pitching on "short rest" when they only get three or four days off in between starts. Hell, Negro League pitchers threw on *no* rest—often after getting little to no sleep following a lengthy ride on a cramped bus.

Negro League starting pitchers usually pitched the *entire* nine-inning game. If it was your game to start, then it was your game to finish. Some Negro League pitchers were such workhorses that they'd even pitch both games of a doubleheader. Larry Kimbrough of the Philadelphia Stars was ambidextrous; he'd pitch the first nine-inning game of a doubleheader right-handed and then the second seven-inning game left-handed (or vice versa). Back then, neither managers nor pitchers were concerned about a "pitch count." If Buck O'Neil would have walked out to the mound to tell Hilton Smith, "I'm taking you out of the game because you're approaching a hundred pitches," Hilton would have popped Buck in the mouth for saying something so insulting.

There was also no such strategy in place to bring in a left-handed relief pitcher to face a left-handed batter; guys in our league were willing to pitch to whatever batter was next on the lineup card. If he got beat, he just got beat. We didn't have "set-up men" and "closers," we just called them "long men," "middle men," and "short men," and they were often the worst pitchers on the team. The guys in the pen didn't pitch that much, because the starters were expected to go all nine.

Now, I realize the game has changed immensely through the years, and that's partly a good thing, but my intent here is to paint a clear picture of just how incredible these players were—and how different the times were as well. The biggest difference I see in the baseball of today compared to baseball "back in the day" is that there was no such thing as a disabled list in the Negro League. If a player was injured, he played hurt. He didn't sit out for 15 days because he had twisted an ankle; he sucked it up and got right back out there. Hell, he better had, or he'd find himself unemployed. Somebody else just as good if not better was always waiting in the wings for a shot. I saw guys hobbling around in so much pain, barely able to walk, that I was hurting for them.

Day after day, these bruised and battered players would perform to the best of their ability. It was nothing to walk out of the umpires' dressing room and see a group of players lined up in the hallway outside their clubhouse, using files to sharpen their steel cleats. On the field, they'd slide into bases feet first, legs swishing about like switchblades, with the intent to slice up anything in their way. If they were sliding into second and couldn't knock down a middle infielder, then they would certainly make him take notice of their spikes. Occasionally, I'd even see a couple of guys slipping rocks into their gloves so that when they smashed their glove across the face of an oncoming runner during the tag, they'd have a much better chance of disorienting him. These guys were fierce rivals and highly competitive.

Understand, this type of trickery wasn't illegal in the Negro Leagues. Like the brushback, it was accepted and common practice, just as it had been for decades. Players, owners, and umpires came to expect it. Fans, of course, craved the aggressive play. Were these tactics unsportsmanlike? Well, yes, by today's standards—but there wasn't anything in the rulebook that said it was prohibited, so umpires never challenged such things in our league. Besides, if you ask me, players nowadays get away with far worse—like steroid use.

The rough play contributed to injuries, and since we didn't have physicians or trainers traveling with the team, the players had to come up with their own home remedies to ease their ailments. They turned to all types of oils, tonics, liniments, and ointments. The combined smells of those concoctions could sure funk up a bus. Sometimes my head would hurt from the mishmash of all the different aromas, which only intensified in a cramped, hot bus.

"Goose grease" was one of the more popular liniments that players used to rub into an injured arm or leg. Goose grease is just what it sounds like it is—the drippings from cooked goose. Older black folks had used this old remedy for decades, so players were quite familiar with its holistic attributes. A hot Epson salt bath was another popular therapy, as was kerosene oil, which black folks referred to as "coal oil." Ball players used coal oil to fight off colds and the flu. A couple swigs of coal oil, combined with a teaspoon of sugar, and a cold would be knocked out faster than Willard Brown could steal home.

In the absence of balms and bandages, a common remedy for healing a deep spike gash was to use the soot from a coal stove, which would stop the bleeding, and then lay spider webs on top of it to seal it. As witch-doctor-y and unsophisticated as all these remedies sound, they worked—or at least we thought they did.

If a player wasn't cutting the mustard talent-wise, or was shucking and jiving around with non-debilitating injuries, then he was dumped. I witnessed such a thing while barnstorming with the Indianapolis Clowns through Ohio one summer. This poor guy reminded me of myself on the pitching mound—he was pitiful. How he lasted for so many games in the Negro Leagues is a mystery to me. Haywood, the fiery manager of the Clowns, pulled one of the cruelest stunts I've ever seen aimed at a ballplayer. One day after this guy had gotten slaughtered in his third or forth outing in a row, Haywood waited until the team bus was out in the middle of nowhere and told the bus driver to stop at a roadside diner so that we could get something to eat. Haywood gave this young boy a wad of cash and told him to go inside and buy sandwiches and drinks for everyone. As soon as that sad sap stepped foot into the diner, Haywood threw the boy's belongings out of the bus and told the driver to "haul ass out of here!" A couple of us stuck our heads out of the window and watched the young man run out of the diner, not realizing what the hell was going on. Haywood later admitted that he gave the kid enough cash to catch a bus back home. But hey, that was life in the Negro Leagues.

Only the strong survived.

IN THE 1950s, WE HAD A HARD enough time fighting to get our players into the majors—let alone managers like Charleston or umpires like me. Sadly, many talented black players fought their way through the Negro Leagues only to get stuck in the minor leagues, or were ignored completely due to the major leagues' unspoken quota of two or less blacks per major league team. To be honest, I don't know if there really was a quota, but there was plenty of talk in the black sports community that major league owners had a secret policy of letting in only so many blacks. Although the Brooklyn Dodgers, St. Louis Browns, and New York Giants were quick to embrace integration, others like the New York Yankees, Philadelphia Phillies, and Boston Red Sox, in particular, took their sweet time in warming up to the idea. The blunt truth of the matter is, every black ballplayer who entered the majors meant one less job for a white ballplayer.

It's important to note that the majors at the time only had 16 teams—eight teams per league—so there was intense competition when vying for those coveted big-league positions. Today there are 30 teams, so all kinds of average talent can slip through the cracks. Not to be crude, but there are guys playing in the major leagues today making millions of dollars who couldn't hold the jockstraps of unsung Negro Leaguers like Sherwood Brewer, Marshall Bridges, Jessie Mitchell, Willie Harris, Pepper Bassett, Verdell Mathis, Lyman Bostock Sr., and Pat Patterson. Compared to what I see on major league diamonds today, I'm here to tell you that *any* of those guys I umpired in the Negro Leagues could have played in the majors today.

The Negro Leagues throughout the 1950s were just as competitive, lively, and exciting as the league had been years earlier. The only difference was in the attitudes of black people in general as we enthusiastically advanced toward integration and equality. To make that leap forward, we let go of what was familiar in the hope of achieving the "American dream." The black business community was hit hard by integration. Black-owned and -operated hotels, restaurants, schools, concessionaries, bus drivers, taxi companies, newspapers, and so forth—which had once thrived—now either fell by the wayside or struggled to simply stay afloat.

But the Negro American League fought to the very end, and fielded competitive, exciting teams. Our community's longstanding love for black baseball was evident on Opening Day of the 1952 Monarchs season. Just as they had done for dozens of years before, on the first day of the new season fans held a parade that started at 18th & Vine (where the Negro Leagues Baseball Museum now stands) and danced and partied all the way to the gates of Blues Stadium, where upwards of 16,000 people crammed through the turnstiles. That same day, on the other side of the state in major league St. Louis, the Cardinals hosted the Cincinnati Reds and only drew about 2,000 people. Looking at the success of the Monarchs that day, and for the remainder of that season, it is clear that people still hungered to see a different brand of baseball. And they got it coming to a Negro League game. There they watched players who had developed a more aggressive playing style, including stealing home, the double steal, the drag bunt, and the hit and run. Black players had redefined the game, adding drama, speed, and motion to the game.

Years later, once I had made it to the Pacific Coast League and saw what was considered the "cream of the crop" of Triple-A ball, I earned a new appreciation for all those talented black players who never got a fair shot. I knew then and I know now that I had been graced by the presence of some of the greatest ballplayers of our time. They were hardly "second rate."

8

I'VE SEEN IT ALL — & THEN SOME

"Just knowing that I was good enough to be there
was the best experience in the world."

* Mamie "Peanut" Johnson, Indianapolis Clowns *

IN 1976, THE MOTION PICTURE *The Bingo Long Traveling All-Stars & Motor Kings* hit theatres throughout the country. On opening night, I excitedly took my family to see what I was sure would be a glimpse into the world of fantastic Negro baseball which I had so frequently told them about. Imagine my disappointment to discover that the movie, although highly entertaining, was more farce than reality.

However, giving *Bingo Long* some benefit of the doubt, yes, there were things that many of us did to entertain the crowds at games; but competitive play, rules, and respect for the integrity of the game always came first. Since this film provided many people with a first glance at the world of black baseball, it's too bad *Bingo Long* didn't accurately portray that aspect of the league. Bingo Long's fictional

All-Stars were loosely based on Satchel Paige's All-Star team. When I say "loosely," I do mean loosely! Believe me, Satchel would have never allowed his team to be as clownish as Bingo Long's.

The Indianapolis Clowns franchise, which prided itself on providing entertainment for fans, was the closest any Negro League team came to Bingo Long's fictional troupe. Three players in particular for the Clowns—Reece "Goose" Tatum, Richard "King Tut" King, and Ralph "Spec" Bebop—were great comic relief for those in attendance. As the designated "clowns," it was their job to entertain; but the other Indianapolis ballplayers were talented players who didn't goof around.

Goose Tatum, definitely the most popular and talented of the clowning triumvirate, was a two-sport athlete, well adept at both baseball and basketball. Although I'd say he was just an above-average baseball player, he was by far one of the best I've ever seen on a basketball court. "The Clown Prince of Basketball," as Tatum was known, also performed with the Harlem Globetrotters. He brought a lot of his Globetrotter gimmicks onto the baseball diamond with the Clowns, where he was a huge drawing card for the Negro Leagues. Fans came just to see what new tricks he would come up with from week to week. In non-league games, Goose would do all sorts of sidesplitting gags for the spectators. His most popular stunt was wearing a grass skirt around his waist—on the field of play—while swaying his hips like a female dancer at a Luau.

Despite his clowning ways, there was no doubting the true athletic ability of Goose Tatum, nor his ability to play baseball. If you'd ever seen him do a summersault flip as a ground ball was zipping his way, watch him field it and then tag the base to get the runner out, then you'd know what I mean. When I was umpiring first base, especially in league games, I always had to keep my eye on Goose. He had the longest arms of any human being I've ever seen, and was crafty enough to try to use them to fool the umpire. Goose knew just how to slap his fist inside his mitt to make it sound as if the ball had gotten to his glove before it actually did. If I wasn't watching the ball closely, his trickery could have made for an embarrassingly incorrect call. He would also carry extra balls in his pockets. Once a runner would take his lead, Goose would pull a ball out and tag him with it in an attempt to fool the runner into believing that he had been tagged out when in fact the pitcher had the game ball. Most runners didn't fall for the gag, but it was good amusement for Goose and his legion of fans.

When he came up to bat, Goose would sometimes try to make the umpire part of the joke. As he would approach the plate he'd bark, "Hey ump, I think that pitcher has done gone an' doctored that ball! Here's a new one." Out of his pocket he'd pull what looked to be a brand-new ball and toss it toward the ump. Oblivious to his gag, the ump would reach out to catch it, but the ball, which was tied to a rubber band, would yo-yo right back to Goose. The ump ended up looking like the biggest imbecile, as the fans roared with laughter. Ol' Goose made me the butt of his jokes on a couple occasions, but luckily I was able to laugh at myself. Goose was a gas, but you had to watch his every move.

I think because I had a sense of humor—which wasn't always true for umpires—Goose began to involve me in his act more and more over time. One of our favorite crowd pleasers involved Goose's ability to juggle. He would ask for three balls, hand one to me, and then start juggling the other two. As the crowd would get revved up he'd say, "Alright ump, hand me that ball!" I would do as instructed and he would proceed to juggle all three—sometimes four—while never missing a beat. While continuing to juggle for several minutes, he would flip one of the balls back to me and have me toss it back to him. The fans hooted and hollered as he'd carry on this routine while walking up and down the base paths, so that everyone could get a good look. I had a good time as his supporting act, but Goose always stole the show.

Richard King, whom everyone knew as "King Tut" because he would occasionally dress in Egyptian garb as part of his shtick, and his sidekick Ralph "Spec" Bebop were also fan favorites. Looking like the chocolate version of comic book duo Mutt and Jeff, Tut and Bebop were a sight to see. Tut, with his long, skinny frame, and Bebop, a midget, thrilled fans and especially children with their silly routines. Their most popular routine was the "row-your-boat" gimmick, in which they pretended to be in a boat. Before games and between innings, Tut and Bebop would perform skits, play shadow ball, and spasm into all kinds of contortions to keep the fans entertained. Tut's claim to fame was batting with a jumbo-sized bat and fielding with an oversized glove (three feet larger than regulation size), which he also used in all types of zany routines.

Tut and Bebop often entered the stands to interact with the crowd, and throughout the game I'd hear the fans howling with laughter. When acting as plate umpire I never turned around to see what was happening, but while umpiring the bases I couldn't help but catch glimpses of their buffoonery. It was sometimes hard for those on the field to maintain a serious demeanor with such antics going on around them. How does an umpire maintain order with these cats clownin' around? It wasn't easy, that's for sure.

On one occasion in Jackson, Mississippi, I saw Tut pick up a little white baby and start parading through the crowd with it. I got a little anxious, thinking the white folks might get their knickers in a twist. Some of the players were feeling the same way, readying their belongings for a quick exit. But being a clown, you can get away with stuff other folks can't. When people started laughing and tossing money into Tut's cap, I had to chuckle myself at his brilliant money-making strategy.

When he wasn't clowning around, King Tut was actually a heck of a ballplayer and could put some serious wood on the ball. I don't particularly think he was major-league caliber, but he was good. Spec Bepop wasn't much of a ballplayer, just an added attraction.

Late in his career All-Star catcher Pepper Bassett joined the clowning brigade when he began catching several innings of a game in a rocking chair! I was caught off guard when, before the start of a Birmingham Black Baron's game, Bassett asked me, "Ump, do you mind if I catch the game sitting down in a rocking chair?" Well aware that the game had probably been advertised featuring the attraction, I consented. The rocker was actually smaller than a standard rocking chair, which made it easy for me to see over it and call balls and strikes. Although it was a novelty, Bassett was adept at catching in that rocker, and I'm sure it was easier on his knees.

A switch-hitting slugger, Bassett had an arm like a rifle and would sometimes mow down base stealers while sitting at the edge of the rocker. Most times, however, he would leap up from the chair and fire a bullet down to second, or pick off a runner loafing at first. If there was going to be a play at the plate, Bassett would kick that rocker out the way so fast you'd think he was kicking shit off his shoes. He'd quickly position himself to make his play, and after dodging the rocking chair I'd be right there on top of the action. Bassett was really an outstanding catcher, truly one of the best in the league. If times had been different, there's no doubt in my mind that he would have found his way up to the majors.

Antics aside, the Negro Leagues contributed more than just a sense of humor to baseball. There were many "firsts" that came out of the league: night games, shin guards, batting helmets, and the team mascot, a distinction held by King Tut. Donning Egyptian attire or odd enhancements to his uniform, he preceded all the furry costumed creatures and signature characters like the Phillie

Phanatic, the San Diego Chicken, the Mariner Moose, Fred Bird, and Billy the Marlin.

TONI STONE, CONNIE MORGAN, and Mamie "Peanut" Johnson broke the gender barrier in the Negro Leagues, providing a unique contribution to the league's history. When I first heard that Syd Pollock, owner of the Indianapolis Clowns, was signing a female player, I thought he was off his nut. But by 1952, the Negro American League was struggling financially and fighting to stay alive. So I guess Pollock, being the brilliant promoter he was, saw the opportunity of signing a woman as great box-office fodder. He was right, for a time.

Women competing alongside men was nothing new in the world of sports, but in the realm of Negro baseball it was definitely an anomaly. In the 1930s, super female athlete Babe Didrikson not only barnstormed with the all-white House of David team, she also played in numerous exhibition games against major leaguers, until the notoriously racist and sexist commissioner of Major League Baseball, Kennesaw Mountain Landis, put an end to it. Another gifted white female athlete, Lizzie Murphy, was also reported to have played against major league All-Star teams, and is credited with having played first base in an exhibition game for the Cleveland Colored Giants when they barnstormed near her Rhode Island hometown in the early 1930s.

Toni Stone was these ladies' black equivalent. Stone shattered the glass ceiling in Negro baseball by becoming the first female to officially become a team member when she joined the Clowns in 1953. Sharing duties with Hank Aaron at second base (she later took over for him), Toni was a tomboyish, average-sized woman who had an aggressive streak and an athletic spirit. Compared to the hundreds of players I'd seen, I thought Toni was just an okay ballplayer. Women at that time did not share the opportunities that men had to compete in sports, so their training as athletes was often behind that of men. So while I can confidently say that the majority of men I umpired in the Negro Leagues could have gone on to play in the majors if given the chance, I can't say the same thing for Toni or the other ladies in the league. But don't get me wrong—if I had to choose three women at that time who I thought could hold their own against men, I certainly would have chosen Toni, Connie, and Peanut. Had they been given the chance, I believe any one of them would have been stars in the All-American Girls Baseball League, which was an actual league featured in the movie *A League of Their Own*. But Jim Crow showed his ugly face as usual and barred black female athletes of that era from participating in the league.

Neither Toni nor Connie had a fluid swing or much prowess at the plate. Peanut was a pitcher, so hitting for average wasn't expected of her. Connie in particular would "chop" at the ball. She relied mostly on her bunting technique to get base hits. Of the three, Toni was by far the best hitter, although she lacked power. She was a contact hitter, capable of plopping the ball over the infield. Where Toni and Connie were of great value to their teams was in the field. Both played second, and they could scoop up ground balls as well as any man. Neither had strong throwing arms, which is probably why they were positioned at second, but they could throw accurately and were relatively quick at turning a double play.

I only umpired one of Peanut Johnson's games. Although she was no Satchel Paige or Booker McDaniel on the mound, she was far better than I. Peanut, nicknamed such by one of her teammates because of her petite size, had a decent fastball and a developing curveball. She was a fierce competitor and adapted well to the art of brushing guys back who had gotten a hit off of her in their previous at-bat. Her aggressiveness aided her in the league, and she held her own most games.

I never saw any evidence of the men in the Negro Leagues being uncomfortable around the women. In fact, the male players were often gentlemen in the presence of these women. Even on the long bus rides in which players usually cut loose, the men toned down their act. If they didn't, they got a subtle reminder from a teammate or a not-so-subtle reminder from their manager. Off the field, the relationship between male and female players appeared to be more sibling-like. On the field, the women were treated fairly, in that they got roughed up right along with the guys. I saw both Toni and Connie get smashed in the face with a glove while sliding into a base, but the same was true for plenty of men. And the girls played just as hard. I'm sure some of the men were trying even harder so they wouldn't get "shown up" by a girl, and the girls were doing their best to keep up with the fellows.

People can debate all they want whether women were used as gimmicks and drawing cards by Negro teams. I choose to stay out of such arguments, because that's not the point. These ladies were pioneering athletes who paved the way for the million-dollar black female athletes of today, like Sheryl Swoopes and Venus and Serena Williams. The modern black female athlete stands on the shoulders of Toni, Connie, and Peanut, whether she realizes it or not.

I am proud to have been a part of a league that excluded no one, unlike many other sports organizations of that era. The Negro Leagues embraced every cross section of society, including whites, Cubans, Puerto Ricans, Mexicans, women, the handicapped, and even convicts, giving them all an equal opportunity to compete on the same playing field with some of the greatest baseball players of our time.

SYD POLLOCK WAS ONE OF the few white impresarios of Negro sports for several decades. As owner of both the Indianapolis Clowns and basketball's Harlem Globetrotters, he certainly did a lot for the black athlete—and made a fist full of money while doing it. Pollock was one of the few owners with whom I was slightly acquainted. I generally made a point not to get involved with owners. Number one, most owners didn't think too much of umpires; and number two, since league president Dr. J. B. Martin was my boss, I didn't want to jeopardize that situation with any type of interference. But I couldn't avoid Pollock. He made his presence known; the man simply would not be ignored.

Pollock was a hustler who could always be found running around the stadium inventing more ways to make money. The guy just couldn't keep still. Like my old umpiring mentor, Frank Duncan, he definitely had the gift of gab. He would go on and on, spewing out more bullshit than a used car salesman. Because of his outgoing personality, he was the kind of guy who would instantly make you feel comfortable, but at the same time make you wonder, *What the hell does he want from me?* But I liked ol' Pollock, mainly because he was always nice to the umpires. The man definitely knew no strangers.

An ace promoter, Pollock kept the Clowns in business longer than anyone expected. His team was geared toward family entertainment, which helped put butts in the seats. After I became a showy crowd pleaser at Blues Stadium with my exuberant calls on the diamond, Pollock asked if I would consider umpiring exclusively for the Clowns and perform more gimmicks for the crowd. Although flattered by the offer, I took my craft seriously, and so I politely declined.

In 1955, during my last "official" year in the leagues, Pollock sold his interest in the Clowns to another white owner, Ed Hamman. The franchise suffered a bit in the transition, but it wasn't for a lack of effort, as Hamman would suit up in a Clowns uniform and help his team entertain the fans. He kept the name and team afloat, and black players employed, well into the 1960s.

The only other team owner I knew peripherally was Ted Rasberry, who was a real card. Loud and gregarious, Rasberry laughed so much that at first I thought something was wrong with him. But the truth is, he was just a happy man who loved life. Rumor had it that Ted had made millions as a gambler, hustler, and numbers banker. I don't know if it was true, but he certainly looked and acted the part, wearing his fedora tilted over his beady eyes and crooked smile. His shifty, fast-talking manner added to the gambler mystique, but Ted was a heck of a nice man and was always genuinely concerned for the umpires' well being. So I had no problem with him.

In the mid-1950s, Ted purchased both the Monarchs and the Detroit Stars. His teams—along with the other two remaining teams, the Clowns and Red Sox—struggled to keep the league alive. Somehow, things stayed afloat until around 1960. I was out of the leagues by then, but I kept tabs on what was going on and rooted for the league's survival.

When I ran into Ted at the 80th anniversary of the Negro Leagues in 2000, I asked the frail yet energetic old man how much he had paid for the Monarchs back in the '50s. Ted snickered and said, "Everybody has asked me that from day one. The answer my brother: more than what I should've, but not as much as I would've!" And knowing Ted, not as much as he *could've*. Anyway, we shared a hearty laugh and left it at that.

WHEN I WASN'T UMPIRING Negro baseball, I occasionally freelanced to make some extra cash. In one such instance, I had the pleasure of briefly traveling with the white House of David ball club. They were a unique group of color-blind young men who treated me no differently than they treated each other. Based out of Benton Harbor, Michigan, the House of David baseball players were representatives of their religious sect of the same name. During the 1930s, the highly competent House of David team made its entrée into the world of Negro Baseball as one of the independent teams that helped sustain black baseball teams that were barnstorming from town to town. Other than a couple of major league "All-Star" teams—including Babe Ruth's and Dizzy Dean's—the House of David was the only all-white team to interact with the Negro Leagues on a consistent basis.

The ballplayers and other men in their sect distinguished themselves by their long hair and beards, which was part of their religious identity. Satchel Paige once said, "They look like Jesus' boys." Upon first seeing them, they seemed relatively intimidating, if not plain old bizarre. But after getting to know them they were some of the kindest, most thoughtful gentlemen I have ever encountered. From what I observed, they were clean-living individuals who (unlike some of the Negro League players) rarely if ever cursed, drank, or chased women. It seemed to me the team's main intent, besides having an athletic outlet for its members, was to raise money for their colony and to use baseball as a vehicle for promoting their religion.

I didn't have to worry about being pressured to become a convert, however. Their sect didn't allow blacks to join. I found this very odd considering how tolerant and open they acted toward blacks. What made their lack of racial inclusiveness even more peculiar was that for a time there was an all-black House of David baseball team that traveled throughout the country as well. Obviously, they were allowed to borrow the name for promotional purposes only. When I traveled with the House of David, I always had to make my way to the black neighborhood and stay in separate housing from the white ballplayers. As a matter of fact, the bus driver usually dropped me off in the black part of town before taking the team on to wherever they were staying.

Once, while traveling with the Monarchs through Michigan, we stopped at the House of David ball field for an exhibition game in Benton Harbor. Although by this time the House of David congregation was in its early waning stage, the compound was still impressive, with acres of land featuring buildings that had once housed everything from a pre-Disneyland-esque amusement park to a zoo; spacious gardens; and a steam locomotive whose track meandered throughout the entire compound. The House of David was a city within a city with every imaginable amenity, apparently necessary to keep its members from pursuing desires in the outside world. Although we weren't allowed to sleep there, we did have an opportunity to walk the grounds of the sprawling estate and take in the sights of this fanciful yet spiritual wonderland.

After seeing how much they valued entertaining their community members, it came as no surprise that the House of David baseball team could be entertaining in its own right. Some of its players performed novelty acts and tricks during games. Similar to the Indianapolis Clowns, they worked in gimmicks to entertain the crowd, including shadow ball and pepper ball, the latter of which they are credited for inventing. Pepper ball—a goofy game where players field a batted ball and then fire the ball back to a batter, who hits the throw back to the fielder at lightning speed—was quite common in the Negro Leagues. The House of David's most famous—and ridiculous—gimmick was playing baseball while seated on mules! But much like the Clowns, at the core of the House of David team were solid baseball fundamentals and a desire to win.

These guys, although not as fit and skilled as the Negro League players, were nothing to turn your nose up at. They could give the best all-black team a run for its money, and won plenty of contests. Even Satchel Paige showed his respect for their athleticism, having spent months touring with the white House of David team during the height of his career in the late 1930s.

Once a thriving religious colony boasting thousands of members, today the House of David sect is only a shell of its former self. The grounds are still there and many of the buildings, although worn and shabby, still stand. The community's once glorious baseball diamond is now a weeded field. If nothing else, the history and contribution of the good-natured gentlemen of the Israelite House of David is well etched in my memory as well as the annals of Negro League history.

9

IT'S HARD OUT HERE FOR AN UMP!

"You cross-eyed old ump,
You're as blind as a stump.
Made me look like a chump,
You horse's rump!"
* From the poem "Yer Out!" by Charles Ghigna *

AFTER BEING NAMED CHIEF UMPIRE by Dr. J. B. Martin, I was given the chance to go on the road with many different teams. I was young and unmarried at the time, so the opportunity to travel across America was exciting for me. But I soon found out that life on the road wasn't a vacation.

Barnstorming, or "road ball" as I called it, had been a staple of black baseball long before the Negro Leagues were formed in 1920. Dating back to the late 19th century, independent black teams "barnstormed" the country, playing exhibition games against both black and white teams. It was a great way for players to supplement their incomes, not only during the season but in the off-season as well. Barnstorming was such big business that stars from both Major League Baseball and the Negro Leagues enjoyed the financial benefits—and the camaraderie—it provided. Imagine today if Albert Pujols compiled a team featuring David Ortiz and Barry Bonds and David Wright and traveled around the country doing battle against the Derek Jeter All-Stars or the Nomar Garciaparra All-Stars. That's the sort of talent some of these barnstorming teams possessed, and why their games turned into huge events for the town lucky enough to host the game.

My brushes with greatness due to my life in the Negro Leagues were numerous, but one of the biggest highlights occurred when I was asked in 1951 to travel to Nashville, Atlanta, and Louisville with Satchel Paige and his All-Stars as they squared off against major leaguer Bob Feller and his team. Although Satchel's team won more games than Feller's, the easygoing camaraderie between the black and white players was evident from the word go. The only color all the players seemed to be concerned with was green. Everyone just wanted to have fun and make some extra cash.

I also had a blast with Roy Campanella and his All-Stars in 1953 as they barnstormed against Negro American League players in a few towns throughout the South. Hearing the players talk about their upcoming tour to the west coast and Hawaii after the southern jaunt was completed made my mouth water. However, it wasn't quite "in the budget" for an umpire to make that trip, so I had to settle for the time I was allotted. Standing on the diamond for those few games with black stars like Don Newcombe, Larry Doby, Monte Irvin, and Hank Aaron—plus Cuban star Minnie Minoso—was an incredible thrill for me. Being chosen to umpire those games was a personal affirmation that I was qualified to make it to the majors. That thrust my drive and determination into high gear.

Campanella was bar none the most talented catcher I ever squatted behind. I had umpired some of the best Negro League catchers: Earl Taborn of the Kansas City Monarchs; Bill "Ready" Cash of the Philadelphia Stars; and Quincy Trouppe, a veteran who during my first season umpiring was on his way out as player/manager of the Chicago American Giants. Campanella had all the qualities of those fine catchers and then some. His quick hands, steady glove, accurate and powerful throwing arm, and willingness to use his body to block the plate made him an exceptional catcher. Runners simply didn't steal on Campy. He could snap off a throw so fast that ball would be waiting at second base for the runner to arrive. And to top it off, he was one of the friendliest men I've ever met. One of the saddest tragedies in baseball history was that horrific car accident that cut short his brilliant career.

Exhibition games like these "All-Stars" games were typically relaxed affairs, so much so that I began to lighten up on my rigid, rules-oriented demeanor and "let my hair down." *Heck, enjoy the atmosphere*, I told myself. Campy and I would often chitchat before games about everything from life in the majors and Negro Leagues to his hobbies of collecting toy trains and gardening. We developed a friendly bond, and by the end of our barnstorming stint I decided to inquire about his willingness to write a letter on my behalf to Major League Baseball commissioner Ford Frick. He enthusiastically obliged, saying, "I don't know much about the umpire world, but I'll be happy to do whatever I can to help you out. Having black umpires would be a great asset to the majors." I also wrote to Mr. Frick myself, stating my credentials in asking for an opportunity to umpire in the big leagues. I thought for sure that by now Major League Baseball could not deny what seemed inevitable to me—that I be the majors' first black umpire. Unfortunately, both of our letters fell on deaf ears. The commissioner never responded. But it was nice to know that for a moment in time, a baseball legend who ultimately became a Hall of

Famer was in my corner, supporting my dreams and ambitions the way no one else had up to that point in my life.

I MOVED ON, DEDICATING MYSELF to my role of chief umpire for the Negro American League. I started by hiring some good umpires to replace the retired Frank Duncan and Wilbur Rogan for the local Monarchs games. I chose George Mayfield of Kansas City and the ever-so-colorful Mark Van Buren of Indianapolis, Indiana. Van Buren was already a seasoned umpire, having spent time in the Negro Leagues as well as one of the Canadian leagues. Mayfield and I had spent time together on the sandlots and in Ban Johnson leagues, so I was familiar with his qualifications. From that point forward, our regular four-man crew consisted of the three of us, plus the ever-faithful Seal Vaughn.

During Monarchs home games at Blues Stadium, Van Buren and I usually traded the hotspots between home and first base. In the major and minor leagues, then and now, all of the umpires rotate clockwise every game. For example, the plate umpire in the first game then moves to third base in the next game, then on to second, and so forth. But in the Negro Leagues we had our own system. The larger-than-life umpires always served as umpire-in-chief (home plate umpire) as a means to entertain the fans. They were usually the more gregarious umpires, and the fans appreciated their over-the-top calls. Mayfield and Vaughn, although solid on the bases, did not have the showmanship of Van Buren or I, so they consistently held down second and third base.

Away from Blues Stadium, I traveled with a two-man crew—usually Van Buren and me. We would pick up a couple umpires once we got to our destination. On average, I spent about 15 days out of each month throughout the spring and summer on the road with various teams. Typically, once we arrived at a stadium, the local umpires would be waiting for me in the umpires' dressing room. After our introductions, we'd discuss specific points like the ground rules and the assignment of bases, and then head to the field. On the occasions when we were playing in smaller towns and no local umpires were available, Van Buren and I would be on our own. I felt at times we even called a better game as a twosome than as a three- or four-man crew. It put added pressure on each of us to cover more ground, but we trusted each other and worked well together, so we made do. Sunday was the one day a week when we could always count on a four-man crew, because Sunday was the big game day in the Negro Leagues. A large turnout of fans was a given, and so was a four-man crew.

Van Buren and I had a great rapport with one another. He was just as energetic and passionate about umpiring as I was, so we made for a good team. Only a few years my senior, he was a handsome, fit, brown-skinned fellow who was just as adept at calling balls and strikes as well as working the bases. I consider him to be one of the closest friends I gained from the Negro Leagues.

EVERY PERSON IN THE NEGRO LEAGUES—whether a manager or player or umpire—had to work side jobs year round to sustain his family. (The one exception was Satchel Paige.) I kept my regular nine-to-five job at General Motors. I was very fortunate with my work situation, because I was allowed flexibility to travel as needed. I never tried to hide the fact that I was an umpire to my employers at GM, and luckily my plant manager was a huge baseball fan and appreciated my passion for the game. So he allowed me to take a leave of absence to follow my main passion. All told, I took plenty of time off in the summer months to barnstorm and never had to quit my job at GM, one that I held for 37 enjoyable years.

On road trips I mostly traveled with the Monarchs since they were my home team. We were never gone for more than two weeks at a time, even though we covered a wide territory and logged a lot of miles on the team bus. The time on the road gave me an opportunity to see thriving metropolises and every little cow town east of the Mississippi. Through the years, I would occasionally switch with another umpire and tour with a different team like the Clowns, Red Sox, or Black Barons, just to break the monotony of being around the same players.

All that time on the road made it difficult to maintain the cardinal rule for umpires: "No socializing with the players." That rule wasn't among The Ten Commandments of Umpiring, but it was an unspoken guideline necessary to maintain the integrity of the game. I decided early on that it would be wise to take up residence in the last row of the bus. Establishing that as my territory ensured that I could hide out in my own world, avoid the temptation of cavorting with players, and most of all keep an eye on the players in case any of them tried confronting me (like in Hank Bayliss' case). It made traveling on the team bus a lonely affair for me. But neither the team nor I could afford to pay for me to travel separately. The league probably could have swung for it, but I don't think they thought enough of the umpires to grant us that luxury. Later, when I umpired in the minor leagues, the rules about fraternizing with ballplayers were very strict and always enforced. Umpires were told that if we boarded a plane or bus and saw a ballplayer or manager from any team, we had to exit immediately and take the next flight or bus—even if it meant risking tardiness for a game.

I preferred when two teams, say for example the Monarchs and Clowns, would hit the road together on a barnstorming tour, because that meant another umpire would be along for the ride. Although Van Buren and I would always have to split up for the bus rides, at least we could shoot the crap with each other when the bus caravan would stop for a rest or a meal. Strength in numbers came in handy, because at times the players would let us have it.

While we umpires were never credited with helping a team win a game, we were often given the credit for a team *losing* one. Boarding the bus I would sometimes hear players bad mouthing me or one of the other umpires. Of course, there were guys who would try to rile me. When I first started road balling in 1950, Memphis Red Sox outfielder Cowan "Bubba" Hyde must have thought I was pretty green. He used to occasionally pick on me, I guess to see how tough the young ump was. He obviously didn't know anything of my background, because if he had, he would have known I was not one to fool with. On occasion, Bubba would come up to me on the bus and question a play that occurred during the game. "Hey ump, was that guy out at second base? What do you think?" he'd ask. Red Sox manager Goose Curry would shout at Bubba, "Quit talking to that umpire—you know better!" Several times on other team buses, managers like Larry Brown, Buck O'Neil, Oscar Charleston, or Hoss Walker would have to occasionally reprimand their players for trying to engage me in conversations or disputes. Players and umpires stayed out of each other's way—especially after ballgames.

Even though it was a lonely way of life, as I look back at those road trips, I don't have any regrets. Just being around those personalities and eavesdropping on their conversations was an absolute gas; so were the experiences I gained traveling from town to town, meeting interesting people, umpiring some incredible ballgames, and learning about life and survival. Barnstorming gave us all a chance to go places and see things we might not have ever gotten to experience otherwise. These were bad times for black folks in many ways, but for us they were also good times.

TO SUMMARIZE MY BARNSTORMING travels, life on the road could be downright brutal. The rides were long, bumpy, and cramped. There is nothing worse than being stuck in tight quarters with a bunch of smelly ballplayers who have just completed a doubleheader on a hot summer day in a stadium that had no shower. I guess I shouldn't complain about the players too much, because most times I couldn't smell them for smelling myself. Since the majority of our games were played on weeknights in the summer months, we'd travel right after a game, sometimes driving all night long to get to our next destination. I recall on some of those trips being stuck in the bus up to 12 hours at a time. Every few hours we'd stop along the way for food, gas, and to relieve ourselves.

We met our fair share of trouble on the road when it came to finding a place to eat. If we were stopping in a major city like Detroit, Memphis, Birmingham, or Miami, I knew I could look forward to sitting down at a black-friendly restaurant and eating a good steak-and-potatoes meal for 50 cents. But in smaller towns, we never knew what might be available to us. If we were scheduled to play an exhibition game against an all-white local team, chances were there was no black community nearby. Unless the white folks decided they were going to accommodate us with food and lodging—which they rarely did—we were shit out of luck. Hungry, tired, and filthy, we'd have to pile back on the bus and head off to the next town. I'm sad to say I can recall a few times having to go days without taking a nice hot bath. On a good day, the first thing I'd do after arriving at a stadium—if there was enough time—was head straight to the black section of town and get something to eat. On some of those long bus rides our lone meal was a baloney and bread sandwich or cheese and crackers. So in those instances, I'd gorge myself at a black restaurant with so much food I felt sick. But that was a good sort of sickness to have.

From town to town, most white crowds were respectful of us because they just wanted to see a good baseball game and marvel at our great athleticism. Of course, we'd always run into a few ignorant kooks who would call us names: nigga, coon, jigga-boo, and spook. Whenever this happened, my mind would flashback to my experiences in the South Pacific. Curious Japanese women and children would run up to us black soldiers and touch our skin to see if the color would rub off. Or they'd walk behind us, pointing and laughing. Those villagers simply wanted to see if what the white American soldiers had told them was true—that Negroes howled at the moon and grew monkey-like tails after the sun went down. My comrades in battle and I just let such nonsense roll off our backs, just as the players and I also did now on the baseball diamonds of America. As a matter of fact, most times we'd get on the bus and have a hearty laugh about it. Those were some of the few times when I shared in bus banter with the players. In those moments, responding to racism, we weren't players and umpires and managers—we were brothers.

The one thing that was really shocking to me was the amount of racial prejudice that I encountered in the North. I was called more names by white people while traveling through the likes of Indiana and Ohio than in Mississippi and Alabama. Leery of every situation, our bus drivers always had the good sense to park the team bus facing outward and toward the parking lot's exit, so that we could get the hell out of Dodge if needed. Fortunately, during my time traveling, a serious situation like that never arose; but it was better to be safe than sorry.

Players kept their minds off racism and their struggles on the road by passing away the time on long bus rides with card games; bid whist, pinochle, blackjack, and poker were the favorites. If the players weren't playing cards, then they were shooting dice, playing dominoes, singing songs, telling nasty jokes, reading, or sharing stories about other players and teams. Some talked about their aspirations to follow Jackie Robinson to the majors. But eventually the talk always came back to a ballplayer's favorite subject: women. Without dropping any names—I wasn't a ballplayer, but I still have respect for that saying, "What you hear in the locker room, stays in the locker room"—I overheard so many sordid details about the sexual conquests of Negro League players I'm almost embarrassed to talk about it. Almost! The guys liked bragging about their successes in the bedroom, and always tried to one-up each other with exaggerated tales. Some had a different girlfriend in every town. Others preferred anonymous one-night stands. Some favored hookers and prostitutes. Still others boasted of having two and three girls at a time. A handful of the players were prudish and completely mum on the subject of sex, but they were definitely in the minority. Most of these guys just enjoyed talking smack. The running joke on one team I traveled with was, so and so "might not have gotten a hit today, but he's gonna get some ass tonight!"

The players' obsession for talking about sex was not contained to the bus; it lingered onto the diamond as well. Sometimes a catcher would try to distract the batter and me by saying something like, "Y'all see that girl over there behind third base? She's got her legs gapped open so wide . . ." While working the bases I would hear a lot more trash talk. Teammates might tell one another, "Hey man, that's the chick over there I was telling you about. I done hit that five or six times!" Another might say, "That broad sitting behind first base has the nerve to be sitting in the front row with no bloomers on!" His teammate might then quip back, "Yeah, you better stop winking at her or I'm gonna tell your wife on you!"

Plenty of women adored the ballplayers, throwing themselves at them wherever we went. Besides the aforementioned antics they pulled in the stands, some women would line up outside the players' entrance as the guys exited the stadium in the hopes of landing a date. Sometimes, when we'd pull up to a ballpark in a new city, girls would be waiting all dolled up and ready to flirt as we stepped off the bus. Manager Buster Haywood was notorious for bounding off the bus with bat in hand, shooing girls away like he was swatting flies. After flailing his Louisville Slugger around, he'd glare and snarl at those poor young gals as if to say, "Now I dare you to mess with one of my players."

BACK IN THE DAY we did all our traveling without the modern convenience of an Interstate highway. Those rickety old team buses—with no air-conditioning or toilets—would chug through back roads to faithfully get us to where we were headed. We entrusted our lives to bus drivers who would somehow navigate, sans a map, what seemed like some of the most far-reaching corners of the country. On exceptionally long rides, certain players and managers would stay up through the night with the driver to ensure he didn't fall asleep. Sometimes a manager or player would even switch off driving duties with the bus driver for a while. Whatever it took, that's what we did to make it to the next day's game. Remarkably, we never missed a game, although we might have shown up an hour or two late from time to time. But the fans and teams would always be patiently waiting, and we'd roll on in and give them a hell of a ball game.

I don't know if some of those bus rides were as grueling as they were just flat out ridiculous. The Memphis Red Sox bus was probably the worst team bus of all. Sam, the driver, would have to stop every 100 or so miles, unload his tools, and fix any number of things—from a dragging tail pipe to a loose fuel pump. As much money as the Martin Brothers apparently had, you would've thought they'd at least buy their ball team a decent bus. But like many team owners, they pinched every penny.

Some team buses were in such disrepair that when going uphill, the driver had to shift into what we called "grandpa gear" (low gear) to keep from putting too much strain on the clutch and brakes. It worked most of the time, but not in the oppressive Florida heat on a Monarchs bus in the summer of 1954. We had just finished a day game and were heading out of Tallahassee, Florida, en route to Miami when disaster struck. As the bus chugged along as usual, we began to smell something burning. I looked out of the window, thinking that a farmer might be burning off crops, when all of a sudden outfielder Herman "Doc" Horn bolted out of his seat and began running up and down the aisle screaming, "We're on fire! We're on fire!"

Now, given these ballplayers' antics over the years and the hysterical (almost joking) tone of Doc's cries, for a split second I thought, *Someone's up to a prank.* That was, until smoke started to engulf the entire bus. Instantly, panic set in and all hell broke loose. Everyone began hollering like a bunch of wild banshees. The driver immediately hit the brakes and skidded off the side of the highway, which put everyone even more on edge. Manager Buck O'Neil, having the good sense to take control of the panic-stricken scene, shouted to everyone, "Get the hell off the bus!" None of us wasted a minute scrambling out that skinny door.

Although we lost clothes, equipment, money, and memories, thank God no one was injured. As we stood on the side of the highway, we watched in total shock as flames engulfed the bus, burning the insides to a crisp. And it all happened in a matter of minutes. It was still daylight, so we were able to flag down some assistance. After a half hour or so the sheriff showed up. Ambling around the outside of our charred bus with what looked like a week-old toothpick wagging in his mouth and a fat black nightstick dangling off his hip, the sheriff assessed the situation, climbed back in his squad car, and promised to send us some assistance "right away." We continued to wait in the blazing Florida sun for a couple hours. None of us could figure out what was taking so long, until infielder Sherwood Brewer admitted to having overheard the sheriff tell the radio dispatcher, "Nothing serious out here. Just a bus burning up with a bunch of niggers on it." Furious, all we could do was sit roadside and wait until another bus happened to drive by.

LIFE IN THE NEGRO LEAGUES was definitely not for the faint of heart. That bus incident was just one of many that I had to deal with while traveling throughout the country. But part of the fun was the challenge of surviving it. Players had to be strong and tough to not only deal with playing games night after night, but also the horrendous travel conditions and the lingering threat of racism. Despite the raucous times we all had on the ball field, there was always the hint of danger that we might run into on the road. America was still grappling with racial issues in the early 1950s, so whether we were in the North or the deep South, we knew to be mindful of our surroundings at all times.

Given my KKK-haunted childhood, I feel very fortunate that I personally never experienced any racial confrontations that were life threatening while on the road. However, other guys throughout the history of the leagues had found themselves in some precarious situations. One chilling story that circulated through locker rooms and on bus rides is that of an early Negro League player from the 1920s who had apparently been caught having sex with a white girl somewhere near Greenville, Mississippi. Legend has it that the player was shot to death and the young lady dragged naked through the city streets and whipped. I wasn't looking to meet such a fate, so

I always minded my Ps and Qs. For the most part, the players I traveled with did so too.

As black people during this time in our country's history, we knew our place. I knew it and every player knew it. As ridiculous and backward as it sounds in this day and age, 50 years ago we did what we had to do and thought nothing of it. It was a way of life we were all used to. Yet there was an unspoken kinship that bonded us Negro Leaguers together through our love of baseball. I believed that if any kind of threatening racial situation ever presented itself, that my brothers would have had my back, as I would have had theirs. After all, we were connected by a mother we called the Negro Leagues, and we were all her children.

I TOLD YOU A GOOD STORY in the first chapter about my near deadly run-in with Monarchs infielder Hank Bayliss on the team bus. Buck O'Neil probably saved my life that night when he broke up the fight and put Bayliss in his place, and for that I am eternally grateful. O'Neil was a real stand-up guy—a class act like no other. He actually came to my aid another evening as well: an evening when anybody else would have told me to go jump in a lake, but not Buck O'Neil.

Buck and I always got along. He rarely argued with me or any other umpire over a call. He was always polite and courteous and often checked in during road trips to make sure the umpire crew had what we needed. During a road game in Jacksonville, Florida, however, Buck and I had one of our few disputes—which we both always chose to recall differently, even though our stories always ended in agreement. Buck always maintained that the play in question involved the infield fly rule; I've always recalled that it was a close call at home plate. Whatever the actual situation was, we were obviously not in agreement. Buck was insistent that I had made a bad call. Totally out of character, he got up in my face during the game and chewed me out. I didn't think much of it and, as usual in those situations, I let the words go in one ear and out the other. After all, this was the good-natured Buck O'Neil. But in this instance, he wasn't so forgiving, uttering the magic words, "You goddamn blind son of a bitch!" That did it—he had to go! So I tossed him.

The story doesn't end there, however. The best part is still to come. Immediately after the game I realized, *Holy shit! I ain't got no place to stay.* The Monarchs' new traveling secretary had either forgotten or hadn't been told to book me a room. I soon discovered that the only black hotel in Jacksonville was sold out for the night, and at this late hour there were no available rooming houses. I had two options: go see Buck and eat a healthy helping of crow, or spend the night on a park bench. I opted to tuck my tail between my legs and get a good night's rest.

Before boarding the bus I explained my situation to Buck. Without hesitation, he responded, "Kid, no problem. Don't worry, you can sleep with me. When we get back to the hotel just tell the desk manager to give you a key to my room." With that he gave me a pat on the back and I boarded the bus. When I got to the tiny little room I was mortified to find only one bed. For a minute I thought, *I'll sleep on the floor*, but there was barely room for that. So I lay down on one side of the full-sized bed and faced the wall, all the while keeping one eye open, waiting for Buck to enter the room. An hour or so later he came in without saying a word. I pretended to be asleep as he got in on the other side of the bed and turned his back toward mine. The next thing I knew he was snoring.

After a good night's rest, I got up early the next morning and hightailed it out of there, happy that he hadn't said anything to me about my call the night before. Obviously, Buck was professional enough to know how to separate life on the diamond from life off the diamond, and not carry a grudge. For that, I am also grateful. The next day it was like nothing had ever happened. Buck was a gentleman, and he never said one word directly to me about that play ever again. He did, however, go on record in several interviews over the years, stating that in his epic baseball career my call that day was the cause of the one and only time he was ever tossed out of a ballgame. Yours truly strikes again!

The last time I saw Buck alive was on September 26, 2006, a week and a half before his death. I had heard that he was not doing well, so I visited him at the hospital. I told my wife before leaving the house that I was going to make him laugh and cheer him up. My plan was to walk into his hospital room and say, "Buck O'Neil, I threw you out of one ballgame, now I'm throwing you out of this hospital. Now, get up out of that bed and go home!" I thought he'd get a kick out of that.

However, upon entering his room, I could see right away that his health had deteriorated so much, and I couldn't bring myself to joke with him. In the 50-some years that I knew him, Buck had always been a larger-than-life personality. His smile beamed bright, his voice boomed, and his eyes twinkled with the joy and wonderment of life. Seeing him lying in that bed, a weakened shell of his former self, was heartbreaking. Our talk that day was all baseball; we discussed the upcoming playoffs (how sweet it would be if Willie Randolph and the Mets could pulled off a World Series victory), and the lackluster season our own Kansas City Royals had endured. Before leaving I gave him a few words of encouragement, a pat on the hand, and the warmest smile I could muster up despite the sadness I was feeling inside.

Buck O'Neil died on Friday, October 6, 2006 at the ripe old age of 94. That day, baseball lost a truly great man and captivating storyteller. I'm honored to have known Buck as a ballplayer, manager, friend, and lifesaver. Shalom, Buck!

BUCK AND BAYLISS WEREN'T the only two people I ever tossed out of a ballgame—far from it. I actually threw out a lot of guys. With a little bit of that military police toughness still running through my veins, I have to admit I loved exerting my power to eject someone who had mouthed off too much or thought he could bully me. I reserved the heave-ho as a last resort, but no one was safe when they crossed the line. (While umpiring in the Ban Johnson League in the 1960s, I threw out my own brother, Don, who was managing one of the teams, for spouting off too much.)

I had made up my mind early on: the umpire controls the game. Once in a while players and managers had to be reminded of that fact—especially in the Negro Leagues. Those players would run all over an umpire if he'd let them. Even fans thought they could influence a game situation with their booing and taunts. It's not so much an issue in baseball today, but 50 and 60 years ago, baseball was a lot less rigid in its structure (especially in the Negro Leagues), so an umpire really had to put his foot down.

When I ejected someone from a game, that player had only so many seconds to get off the field. If he didn't comply, then I'd threaten to forfeit the ballgame. I never had to actually follow through on the threat, although I did come close a couple of times. I thought nothing of telling a player, "I'm gonna give you ten seconds to get off this field or I'm forfeiting the game." Then I'd start counting. Most guys would storm off while still giving me a tongue-lashing; others were more defiant and liked to see just how much they could get away with. I sometimes cut a bit of slack to the more mild-mannered guys who didn't give me grief too often. But they were the exception. If ever I had a major issue, like in Hank Bayliss' case, I would always call Dr. Martin to inform him of what had happened. He was well aware of the often-treacherous plight of umpires, so he always encouraged me to check in with him from time to time to let him know how things were going.

Of all the Negro Leaguers who enjoyed pestering me, Indianapolis Clowns manager Buster Haywood used to give me the blues more often than anyone else. I think Haywood missed playing the game so much—he had been a star catcher as a player—that he used the umpires as targets, giving us a tongue-lashing to keep his face in front of the fans. He would sometimes argue with me over the silliest calls. He was brazen, too—kicking up dirt onto the bases, yelling into my ear with his lips just centimeters from my earlobe, and jumping up and down like a child throwing a tantrum. When he really wanted to be dramatic in his protest, he would fall to the ground and scream at the top of his lungs. Haywood was ahead of his time, a real Earl Weaver or Billy Martin when it came to letting the umps have it. The fans loved his outbursts, and he loved giving them a show, much like some of his Clowns players.

During his tirades I would have to tell him sternly, "All right Haywood, you can kick up all the dust you want to, but the second you kick some up on me I'm yanking you out of here." Oh, he'd really cut up then, kicking and fussing like a crazed lunatic. I'd sometimes have to bite my lip to keep from laughing at his antics. I'm sure he knew I was getting a kick out of him, too, because he would put a little extra zip in his act. To his credit, though, even with all his frequent rages, I can only recall two times that I had to throw him out of a game.

One particularly memorable Haywood moment came when he was managing the Memphis Red Sox. I got so mad at him that I cleared his *entire* team bench! It wasn't the first time I had felt the need to remove an entire squad; I had also done it to the Monarchs and the Black Barons because they had gotten so out of line. But that time was the most memorable. Haywood had snapped off one of his typical insulting barbs from the dugout, and this time it really got under my skin. I marched over to the dugout and told him dead straight, "I want everybody off this bench, Haywood. I ain't dealing with your mouth today. When I get back to the plate and turn around I don't wanna see nobody sitting here but you!"

Haywood thought I had lost my mind, but it got his attention. "Motley, you're crazy! You can't clear my bench," Haywood snapped. I had to fight against every nerve in my body in order to bite my tongue and not curse his soul. I shot back, "You heard me, Haywood! I want them out of here!" Haywood knew I was dead serious and immediately changed his tune. "Motley, where they supposed to go? This goddamn stadium ain't got no locker room." Not letting up, I dug my heals in, "I don't care where they go. Send them to the bus if you have to. All I know is I don't want to see no one's butt but yours on this bench!" By the time I reached home plate and turned around, Haywood was sitting alone, looking like a mother hen whose chicks had just been eaten by the big bad wolf.

Haywood later got his revenge in the most humorous fashion. During an exhibition game I was umpiring with the Clowns in Toledo, Ohio, Haywood and I began a routine that was to become a trademark for us for years. Umpiring first base, I called out a Clowns runner who had gotten picked off of first. Haywood came barreling out of the dugout and started in with his usual outburst. I rolled my eyes and as usual, began to walk away from him. At first he was serious in his protest, but as the crowd started reacting to him, Haywood lurched at me, just inches from my face and said, "Motley, can't you see how much these people are loving this?" Still waving his arms and shaking his head as if he was arguing, he continued, "Act like you're arguing back with me. Just work your mouth!" And with that, I got in on the act. There we stood, toe to toe, mouth to mouth, yelling nonsense at each other as if we were ready to snap each other's neck off. Haywood could have kept it going for hours. Finally, after a couple minutes, I could hardly contain myself from laughing out loud. I told Haywood, "All right, we've had our fun, now go sit down."

After that day, Haywood and I began a regular shouting routine much to the delight of fans all across the country. We only acted out if the game's decision wasn't in doubt. Fans always thought we were dire enemies because we "argued" all the time, but that couldn't have been further from the truth. I had a lot of respect for Haywood, even though his antics sometimes overshadowed his genius for managing the game. He was an extremely knowledgeable skipper and knew exactly how to get the best from his players.

Since guys in the Negro Leagues showed no mercy to the umpire, the umpires had to fight fire with fire. I think players sometimes liked to mess with me in particular because they knew they'd get a reaction. Oftentimes players would curse me from the bench, knowing I couldn't tell exactly who was the culprit. I soon learned how to deal with this problem. Since I wasn't sure who the guilty party was, I'd go over to the bench and pick out the quiet, well-behaved guy on the team (who I knew was innocent) and I'd throw *him* out. One time, a poor Philadelphia Stars player was almost in tears after I tossed him, whimpering, "But umpire! I didn't say nothing!" I snapped right back, "You just did, now get out of here!" I knew good and well he hadn't said a word, but I had to make my point with his teammates. Sometimes it worked, sometimes it didn't.

I made my point one day with Monarchs player Francisco "Pancho" Herrera, one of the many Cuban-born athletes who played in the Negro Leagues. Like many catchers do, Pancho would try to trick me after catching a pitch by moving his glove ever so slightly into the strike zone. I had become used to this trick and was certainly not falling for it. On one particular call

Pancho decided to challenge me in his native tongue. Since I didn't speak Spanish, there was really nothing I could do about it. I tried ignoring him at first to give him the benefit of the doubt. I remember telling him, "You can rant and rave all you want, but you're not changing my mind." But then after a few seconds my instincts told me, *This fool is cussing me out in Spanish.* He should have quit while he was ahead, but instead he kept rambling on. My ears perked up as he began to interject a few heavily accented yet all too familiar English words. In his broken English, I heard him mutter, "Joo stoo-peed ay-ass-ol!" As I snapped around and looked him in the eyes, he zipped his lips, looking like a deer caught in headlights. Knowing what was coming next, Herrera turned toward the dugout, making an effort to upstage me before I tossed him from the game. It was too late: I barked in my best Spanish accent, *"J-O-O OUTTA H-E-E-R-R-R-R-E!"*

IT WAS PRETTY COMMON in the Negro Leagues for a team or a player to retaliate against an umpire if they felt he had made a poor call. Players used to slide wide of the bag and barrel right into the umpire, spiking him out of spite due to a call they disagreed with. If the catcher didn't like the way an umpire was calling balls and strikes, he would purposely let a pitch go by so it would smack the umpire right in the facemask. That happened to me at least half a dozen times. Of course the catcher would then apologize profusely, trying to act as if he had just misjudged the ball. But it was always obvious when he had done it deliberately, so I'd eject him. One time after I threw out Memphis Red Sox catcher Casey Jones for pulling this stunt, Buster Haywood had the nerve to come out to question why I was tossing his catcher. So just to get his ire up for asking such a dumb question, I tossed out his pitcher, too.

When you get hit in the throat, chin, forehead, or face by a 90-some-mile-an-hour fastball, believe me, you know you've been hit. The facemask doesn't help all that much. It stings much worse than a foul tipped ball because it's a direct hit. The masks we wore back then weren't nearly as sturdy as they are now. I had one such throw in which the baseball actually got lodged in the grill of my mask. Another time the ball broke through my mask and struck my cheekbone. Thank God the mask bore the brunt of the impact before the ball slipped inside.

Players in the Negro Leagues were a handful to deal with, but they were a cakewalk compared to the fans. Fans could be relentless, often showing no mercy to umpires. So at least that much hasn't really changed over the years. Negro League fans loved razzing the umpires, even on routine plays. One minute they'd applaud an umpire for making a good call (especially if he put a little extra zip in his hip); then they would turn on him a minute later if they didn't like a call he had made.

In a few cities like Birmingham, Indianapolis, and Cincinnati, the fans had created a little taunt they chanted that was a crowd favorite: "Kill the umpire! Kill the umpire!" The chant got crowds so worked up into a frenzy that it was almost hard to hear myself think. The organist would add to the madness by pounding out a weird dirge that got the entire stadium chanting in unison. It was unnerving at first, but I quickly realized that it was just all part of the fun game experience for most fans. Some crazy fans, however, took that chant to be a literal declaration. After playing a game in Birmingham, our umpire crew came out of the stadium after a game only to find that the car we were riding in had been turned upside down by disgruntled fans. Blaming us for the loss suffered by their Black Barons, some mischievous fans decided to take their angst out on us umpires.

Several times when crowds were really pissed off about a loss, the umpire crew would have to wait for the entire stadium and parking lot to clear before exiting. We didn't want to take any chances. In one particular game at my beloved Blues Stadium in Kansas City, I found out just how intense the wrath of Negro League fans could get. All I remember is that on the last out of the game, 15,000 Monarchs fans decided at once to blame Bob Motley for the team's loss. All of a sudden a sea of Coca-Cola bottles started raining down from the stands—all aimed at me. I was nailed a couple times, as were some of the players who didn't have a chance to run off the field to safety. I remember Buck O'Neil and Oscar Charleston—the managers that day—running for their team's dugout, and one of them shouting to me to head for second base, out of the reach of the bottle-tossing mob in the stands. (In hindsight, I'm not sure why I didn't run for the dugout as well.) The bottles kept coming by the dozens from all directions, and within minutes the field was littered with them. Fearing an out and out riot, Buck and Charleston left the safety of their dugouts and escorted me all the way to the center-field wall, where we made an escape. How the three of us scaled that wall is still a mystery to me, but we did.

True to the spirit of Negro League competition, the following week all order was restored at Blues Stadium and all transgressions forgotten and forgiven. Everyone acted as if nothing had ever happened. In all honesty, that was the only time I had been really fearful of fans, but I always knew to keep my wits about myself in dealing with them—just in case. If someone approached me after a game and asked, "Hey, weren't you one of the umpires?" I'd calmly answer back, "No, I'm a spectator like you." A couple of times I even added, "If you see that bastard let me know 'cause I'm looking for him, too!"

One thing about Negro League fans: they never blamed their team for a loss. That distinction either went to the opposing team—a cheating player was often the culprit—or the umpire.

One of their players could have bobbled a ball or made an errant throw to cost his team the game, but the fans would find some reason to blame someone else. Still, Negro League fans were the greatest fans in the world. They were devoted, passionate, and fanatical. In short, they *loved* baseball and their home team. They enjoyed every aspect of the game, and that included far more than just the ballgame itself. Dressed up in their finest attire, fans enjoyed everything from the tailgating-like picnics held at games to the carnival-esque atmosphere of pregame activities such as concerts and beauty contests that different teams provided as entertainment. People came out to enjoy a full day of fun at the ballpark.

Even on occasion, when the fun had been sucked out of the ballpark, Negro League fans showed their true spirit. One of the strangest games I was ever involved in was a night game in Cocoa, Florida, between the Monarchs and Black Barons. The game, a sellout as usual, was supposed to start at 7 p.m., but torrential rains had delayed the start of the game. Being chief umpire, it was my responsibility to make the decision on canceling the game. After waiting an hour, I could see there was no end in sight to the heavy downpour. But since this was a one-night affair, the promoters insisted that we "wait a little longer," since canceling the game meant they'd have to refund the ticket money. Finally, the rains subsided around midnight. As you can imagine, the field was completely soaked, but those Floridians must have been used to dealing with such conditions, because what I saw next was something I'd never seen before. The grounds crew came in with gasoline and poured it all over the diamond, then torched the field to burn off the wetness. Surprisingly, the field—although somewhat moist in some areas—was soon dry enough to play on. The game finally commenced at 1:30 in the morning. After all that time spent waiting in the rain, about 20 diehard fans still remained, ready for some baseball. Drenched and happy as clams, they sat through the five innings that were played in order to make it a "complete game."

The reason fans were so passionate about Negro baseball was simple: in Negro League players they found heroes whom they could worship. As far as sports figures were concerned, there were only a handful of famous black athletes during the heyday of the Negro Leagues: Joe Louis, Jack Johnson, and Jesse Owens. There were also few political leaders; fewer successful businessmen or women; and even fewer professionals such as lawyers, doctors, or dentists within the black community. So ballplayers and musicians—along with clergymen and schoolteachers—were the role models and icons for most black Americans. That is why I believe, even today, sports and entertainment are a big part of black culture. To drive that point home, on Sundays when a Negro League game was scheduled, black preachers would cut short their sermons because they knew that come 11 a.m. the entire congregation was going to start filtering out, making a mass exodus to the ball field for the noon game. This tradition was longstanding and demonstrates the impact of the Negro Leagues on black culture.

Unlike today, it was rare in my time to hear a fan bad mouth a Negro League player, especially one of the hometown guys. Fans were loyal and supportive to the bitter end, holding players—even opponents—in high regard. Interestingly enough, women were more fanatical about the game than men. Women came in droves and were always dressed to kill in their sundresses, flowery hats, and high-heeled shoes. In the days preceding a big Sunday game, beauty shops would give discounts to women so that they could get their "do's" done before for the big day. Walking down 18th & Vine in Kansas City or Main & McCall in Memphis on a Saturday before a home game, I could practically smell all the hair burning from the hot combs and curling irons that beauticians used to style hair.

Yes, the women were dedicated supporters. During games, I was called a "no-good umpire" or "blind bat" by more women than men. A buddy of mine told me once about catching the fury of a group of women in the old Blue Room tavern in Kansas City for bad mouthing the Monarchs after a game. They were eager to defend their team: they beat him—not brutally, but enough that he never said another negative word about the Monarchs in public again. I made sure to follow suit and keep my mouth shut.

10
THE LOOK OF LOVE

"Without true love, we just exist."
* Lyrics by Hal David, from the song "Alfie" *

BY THE SUMMER OF 1952 I had met a cute little girl from Sioux City, Iowa, and decided to marry her. I met Ms. Edna Pearline Hayes at Kansas City's Municipal Auditorium during a dance concert by the famous rhythm and blues band leader Louis Jordan. An extraordinary showman who was known for such party favorites as "Saturday Night Fish Fry," "Ain't Nobody Here But Us Chickens," "Beans and Corn Bread," and "Caldonia," Jordan was the favorite musical act of many young black hipsters at the time. Jordan's music jumped, and we all enjoyed tapping our feet, snapping our fingers, bouncing, and boogieing right along.

For weeks I had been anticipating this night. Not being much of a dancer, I nearly threw my back out practicing the "Lindy Hop," the "Shorty George," and the "Snake Hips" by myself in front of the mirror in my tiny apartment. If anyone had walked in on me practicing they would have surely thought I was crazy and put me in the nut house. But by the time that concert arrived this cat was ready to cut a rug. Clean as a chitlin', I was looking spiffy and smelling fine!

Dapperly dressed in my new *"fit-out"*—black, patent leather Stacy Adams shoes, tan shirt, black slacks, multicolored tie, black jacket, and stylish black pork pie hat—I was determined to "shake a tail feather" and case the joint to try to catch the eye of some pretty young thing. Arriving fashionably late, or on "CP time" (Colored People's time) as we called it back in the day, I had no more than opened the door leading to the arena foyer when two girls with pumps in hand scurried past, pushing me out of the way in their attempt to exit. Out of breath and shaking slightly, both girls had panic-stricken looks on their faces. Sauntering behind them and looking very much annoyed was my friend, Ella Mae Searcy. I was anxious to get inside as I could hear Louis Jordan and his band "letting the good times roll" just on the other side of the arena doors; but being the nosey sap that I am, I stopped Ella Mae to see if there was some kind of trouble.

"Ella Mae, do you know those girls?" I asked.

"Uh-huh, and they are working my *very last* nerve!" Ella Mae responded huffily.

"What's going on? Why are they running out?" I asked. "Them niggas ain't starting to act a fool up in there, are they?"

Ella Mae rolled her eyes in disgust. "Uh-uh," she sneered, *"they're scared!"*

"Scared?" I asked, puzzled. "Scared of what? They look they've just seen a ghost."

Ella Mae shot back, "The only ghosts these fools have seen are them 10,000 spooks in there partying! They're from Iowa. They ain't never been around this many black folks before and are nervous as all get out. Can you believe that shit?"

I nearly fell over laughing. Ella Mae was not amused. As the four of us stood outside the auditorium, Ella Mae and I tried, with no success, to coax the overwhelmed young ladies back inside. Finally tired of arguing, Ella Mae asked if I would "be a dear" and give them all a lift home. Disappointed that I wasn't going to get a chance to try out my well-rehearsed moves to the music of my favorite musician, I reluctantly agreed. As it turns out, it was the best decision of my entire life.

Once in my car, the out-of-town girls relaxed, and I was able to find out a little more about them. Pearline and her friend Maxine Taylor had just graduated from high school, and their parents awarded them with trips to Kansas City to visit Maxine's cousin, Ella Mae. Interestingly enough, Maxine made sure that she sat in the front seat. I later found out that she was "digging my scene" and had sat up front so that she could flirt with me. While Maxine blabbed on about nothing in particular, I turned my attention to the cute high yella' gal in the back. Seemingly unimpressed and uninterested in me, Pearline sat stoically behind my seat and gazed out of her window at the limited sights of the dark night. Ella Mae, on the passenger side of the back seat, sat there with her mouth poked out, pissed that she had been coerced into leaving the dance early. Playing the part of the smooth Casanova, I positioned my rear-view mirror so that I could see Pearline in the mirror's reflection. Every time she glanced my way, I'd wink at her. Each time, she'd bashfully turn away as if she didn't notice. Since I was seemingly getting nowhere with my winks and had little desire to take the girls all the way to Ella Mae's house outside of town, I decided instead to take them to Frank Duncan's taxi stand near 18th & Vine and pay for their taxi ride home.

Later that night, I was unable to get the little gal from Sioux City off my mind. Knowing she would soon be returning home to

Iowa, I decided to get to work—and fast. So bright and early the next morning I called Ella Mae to see if she could possibly arrange a date for me that night with "the cute yella girl." Not wanting Ella Mae or Maxine to feel slighted, I arranged blind dates for both of them with my most handsome buddies, Charles White and Wade Hartso. Ella Mae and Wade hated each other from the word jump, but Maxine and Charles hit it off immediately and enjoyed a lengthy courtship. As for Pearline and I, we married a year later. My attempt at playing Cupid paid off well—two out of three ain't bad! Pearline and I have been going strong for nearly 55 years.

After that first date, I began a long-distance courtship with Pearline. I would drive the 300 miles of non-Interstate roads to Sioux City to visit her once a week. When her parents could make sure that she was duly chaperoned, she was allowed to visit me in Kansas City. She came to watch me umpire at Blues Stadium, and I made sure I really showed out. After all, a man knows he's got to impress his lady. I was kicking, shouting, twisting, leaping, doing the splits—you name it. Of course she loved it.

In time, I'm happy to report that my new Iowan bride became more and more accustomed to being in the company of 10,000 or more Negroes, primarily because of all those Monarchs games she attended. But it took her years to get used to the concept of a segregated Missouri. Having spent her life in a totally integrated society, the idea of blacks and whites living separate from one another was totally foreign to her. It was shocking for her to learn of my KKK-infested upbringing in the South, just as it was eye opening for me to learn that black folks of my generation could live another way in America.

After our marriage, leaving for long barnstorming trips became more challenging for me, especially after our first child, daughter Bobette Jane, was born. I was still technically employed by General Motors, but I was taking lots of time off for my umpiring. The $300 a month I was earning in baseball could scarcely support my travels *and* my new family back home. Times were tough, but thankfully I had married a woman who was supportive of my every dream and encouraged me to stick with baseball. So I stuck with my plan of one day umpiring in the majors.

11

THE EAST-WEST CLASSIC

"You can take Ziegfeld's Follies and Barnum's Great Shows
and roll 'em into one. You can have the World Series or a
Joe Louis fight, with its action, drama and fun. But for me
my dear friends there's only one show and it's greater than all
of the rest. It's that stupendous, gigantic, colossal attraction
when the East locks horns with the West!"

* Wendell Smith, Pittsburgh Courier *

ONE OF MY LONGTIME GOALS was to be a part of the annual East-West All-Star game. More significant than any opening day or even the Negro Leagues' World Series, the East-West game was *the* event in all of black baseball. Debuting on September 10, 1933 (two months after the major league's All-Star game premiere), the East-West game was the brainchild of Gus Greenlee, the owner of the legendary Pittsburgh Crawfords and one of the kingpins of East Coast black baseball. The East-West classic, held annually at Chicago's famed Comiskey Park, eventually grew to be such a spectacle that people from all around the country attended the event. It was a celebration like no other I have ever witnessed in my life.

The game marked the crowning achievement for black players and umpires in the Negro Leagues. Adapting to the system used by the majors, the black press—from the *New York Amsterdam News* to the *Baltimore Afro-American* to the communist rag the *Daily Worker*—provided ballots in their newspapers so that fans could select their favorite players from the American and National Leagues. The *Chicago Defender* and the *Pittsburgh Courier* were responsible for tallying the votes and announcing which players were participating.

When you had been voted in as a player, you had arrived and were deemed a star. When you were asked by the league president to umpire, you were validated as one of the league's best. When as a fan you could you see all of your heroes in person under one roof, you were mesmerized—thrilled beyond belief. Yes, the East-West game was a big deal. Names of Hall of Famers such as Josh Gibson, Buck Leonard, Leon Day, Willie Wells, Monte Irvin, Cool Papa Bell, and Satchel Paige graced the big game's box score for over 20 glorious East-West encounters. In the days before television, this was the only opportunity for a fan to see all the greats, and so fans flocked to the event. From its inception, the black All-Star game consistently outdrew its major league counterpart up until the mid-1950s, when the Negro Leagues were struggling to stay afloat.

The East-West competitions were always fiercely fought battles. Unlike Major League Baseball's All-Star game, this was not an exhibition game where players were rotated in every few innings as a goodwill gesture to give everybody an opportunity to play. No way: for black players, the East-West game is what separated the men from the boys. Everybody was out to win and show the fans, sportswriters, owners, and each other just what they were made of. Players were out for blood, and their skippers managed accordingly.

For fans, the event was a chance to be among greatness. Money would be saved for weeks in advance to purchase round-trip train fares, hotel rooms, new outfits, and weekend babysitters. From Thursday afternoon until Monday morning every juke joint, night club, and tavern up and down Chicago's Halsted Street would be bursting at the seams with sharply dressed black folks who had come in from as far west as California, as far east as New York, as far south as New Orleans, and from every point in between. Around Kansas City, and I'm sure the rest of the country as well, folks talked about the game nearly year-round. That's just how important the games were to us. Hell, look at me—I'm *still* talking about it!

Black celebrities used the East-West games as promotional fare as well. Through the years it was common to see the likes of Lena Horne, Bill "Bojangles" Robinson, Hattie McDaniel, Joe Louis, Lionel Hampton, Count Basie, Cab Calloway, and a slew of other black stars either in attendance or participating in the pregame festivities. The East-West spectacle was definitely the place to see and be seen.

After settling down in Kansas City, I fell so in love with Negro League ball that I decided to venture to Chicago to see what all the fuss was about. In 1947, because two former East-West alums, Jackie Robinson and Larry Doby, had kicked down the door to the majors, rumors were running rampant that the Negro Leagues were folding and that this would be the final year for the East-West game. I decided I could not miss out on the chance to witness the affair for myself. My train ride on the Santa Fe Chief from Kansas City to Chicago was one great big party. The compartments were packed with black people of every hue going northward for one purpose, the All-Star game. The traditional theme song on those train rides was Count Basie's hit song "Goin' to Chicago Blues." When the feeling hit us, the all-black sections of the train would break into an impromptu, a cappella rendition of the song. Oh we had a time! I'm sure the white passengers up in their segregated compartments didn't know what the hell was going on.

Although I would have gladly paid the three bucks admission, I was lucky enough to get a complimentary ticket to the 1947 game through a co-worker's cousin who lived in Chicago. Walking into Comiskey was like walking into a dream. It was an unbelievable feeling that still gives me goose bumps when I think back on it. The huge stadium was filled to capacity with around 50,000 well-dressed, die-hard black baseball fans. It was a perfect July day: clouds filtered the sky, and the temperature was a comfortable 85 degrees.

As the players were introduced and lined up along the base lines, I was enthralled by the colorful display of the different uniforms of each participating team, including the Baltimore Elite Giants, Newark Eagles, Homestead Grays, Cleveland Buckeyes, New York Cubans, New York Black Yankees, Birmingham Black Barons, Philadelphia Stars, Indianapolis Clowns, Memphis Red Sox, Chicago American Giants, and, of course, my hometown Kansas City Monarchs. The players represented were the greatest black professional athletes of our day: Monte Irvin, Henry Kimbro, Minnie Minoso, Dan Bankhead, Artie Wilson, Sam Jethroe, Piper Davis, Quincy Trouppe, Gentry Jessup, Max Manning, Silvio Garcia, Pee Wee Butts, and Luis Tiant Sr. Even Goose Tatum was there, entertaining the crowd with his usual clownish antics. I was shocked to see not four, but six umpires on the field: one on each base and one down both the left and right field lines. I had seen the six-umpire system used at the Monarchs-Eagles World Series game the previous year, but its presence at the East-West game was more intriguing to me because it proved how seriously the game was taken.

The West team—who I considered "my guys," since Kansas City was represented—came out on top with a 5-2 victory over the East. The play was fiercely competitive and outstanding as usual. It was a memorable afternoon, well worth the $20 roundtrip train ticket—especially if I had indeed seen the last of the great East-West games. But lo and behold, despite the predictions of cynics, Negro baseball was still around in 1948, and would persist for 12 more seasons after that. Although attendance decreased more and more each year, many loyal followers of black ball hung in there until the bitter end.

LITTLE DID I KNOW that 1947 day that I would have the opportunity to umpire the East-West All-Star game four times! The 21st, 22nd, 23rd, and 24th annual classics—from 1953-1956—were the highlights of my umpiring career. I was treated like royalty at each, given roundtrip train fare, a great hotel room at Chicago's all-black Grand Hotel, and car service in a brand-spanking new automobile, plus $50 in my pocket as my pay for the day.

Visiting Comiskey Park was one thing; actually walking onto the hallowed grounds of the park was another—a spine-tingling, awe-inspiring experience. One of the most historic of all ballparks, Comiskey was an olden jewel. My first year I relished every moment, not knowing if I would ever be asked to do it again. I arrived good and early to prepare for the game and to commune with the spirits of Comiskey. While the players were preparing for batting practice, before fans were let into the ballpark, I made a beeline to the field to soak it all in. I was so elated to be standing on the Comiskey diamond that I rolled around on the grass like a little kid making snow angels. I was beaming from ear to ear with joy, to the delight and bewilderment of many of the players. But I didn't care; I was one step closer to umpiring in the big leagues—or so I thought.

I love experiencing new baseball stadiums—always have, always will. I first performed my ground-rolling ritual at my Comiskey debut, and did it again the following two years at the East-West games. When I umpired my one and only game in Boston's Fenway Park in the early 1950s, I did it there, too. As a way of saying goodbye to Blues Stadium in its final days before it was demolished in the 1970s, I did it again. During the 1960s on a trip to New York City with my family, I somehow managed to get us into Yankee Stadium and onto the diamond while the team was away on a road trip. I did it there, too. My wife and kids were mortified, but again, I didn't care!

Having been in the stands at Comiskey a few years prior, I was now front and center at the biggest event in the world of Negro sports. The stadium, though not as packed as it was in 1947, still held close to 20,000 people. I had worked in front of big crowds before, but this was so thrilling I could hardly stand still. I served as umpire-in-chief for the six-umpire crew, calling balls and strikes. The league had appointed various other umpires from around the country, including T.H. Jefferson, Simon Lewis, Ted Acklyn, Earl Vann, and my buddy Mark Van Buren. Unfortunately by this point in the league's history, the once prosperous Negro League had now diminished to only four competing teams, and it was hardly an accurate representation of "East" versus "West"; the Kansas City Monarchs and Memphis Red Sox represented the West, while the Birmingham Black Barons and Indianapolis Clowns represented the East.

The stands were crawling with white major league scouts who knew this game would provide a peek at the best the league had to offer. Every player used this opportunity to audition for the majors. Even though a foreseeable end of an era was staring us in the face, for the time being there was still hope in the air that Negro baseball just might survive. The *Kansas City Call* even predicted, "The 21st annual East-West All-Star game which will be played here in Comiskey Park on Sunday, August 16 looms as a classic performance comparable to the old days. . . . [The] chief reason for the prediction of a gigantic struggle is the extraordinary high caliber of talent that has been concentrated into four clubs of the Negro American League."

Excitedly, I took in every moment of that glorious day. The pregame activities were festive. A marching band hammered out a highly energized high-stepping routine while the Flying Nesbitts, the only all-black acrobatic-comedy troupe at the time, wowed the crowd. Most exciting for me, however, was a chance to see my old mentor, league president Dr. J. B. Martin, whom I had not seen much since our initial meeting in 1950. After he caught the ceremonial first pitch thrown out by John H. Sengstacke, editor and publisher of the *Chicago Defender*, I loudly and proudly shouted, "Play ball!" Shaking Dr. Martin's hand at that moment was as satisfying and affirming a moment as I experienced in my life.

Buck O'Neil's West team came out victorious again with a 5-1 defeat of Buster Haywood's East team, improving the West's record in the classic to 13-8. Some of the standouts from both squads included Pee Wee Butts, Ray Neil, Henry Kimbro, Doc Dennis, Carl Long, Pepper Bassett, Sherwood Brewer, and Ray Haggins. Even my old nemesis Hank Bayliss made an appearance. Disappointingly, my "Shiner," Ernie Banks, went 0-4 in the game and didn't turn one of his signature double plays.

On August 22, 1954 I found myself back at Comiskey for the 22nd annual contest, once again serving as umpire-in-chief in a game won by the West, 6-4. Stripped of its characteristic "East-West" moniker due to the lack of actual teams from the East, the contest was now officially renamed the "Negro League All-Star Game." Six teams now graced the league; in addition to the four

1953 teams, the Detroit Stars and Louisville Black Colonels had made entrances as new franchises into our fading league. Only about 10,000 spectators dotted the massive stadium—indeed a far cry from the 50,000 who had attended a few years prior—so the major league All-Star game finally got its wish and outdrew our classic in attendance. By that point, they should have been outdrawing us, since they had a majority of our best players.

I elected to start the 1954 game at home plate, where I umpired the first five innings before rotating with the infield umps for the sixth through ninth innings to give each the opportunity to be behind the plate as well. We all reluctantly sensed that the end was inevitable, so it seemed the only fair thing to do. As if to underline our impression that the league was finally on its way out, just two months after the game, Oscar Charleston, who in 1954 had piloted the East team and led the Clowns to the Negro League title, died suddenly at the age of 57. His untimely death sent shockwaves through the world of black baseball and marked the end of a great era for the Negro Leagues. In his popular *Chicago Defender* sports column, noted sportswriter Frank "Fay" Young wrote of Charleston: "The death of Oscar Charleston removes from this green earth the greatest all-round Negro ball player of all times."

I was pleased to be invited back by Dr. Martin to umpire the All-Star game in 1955 and 1956. I didn't know it at the time, but '56 would be my final appearance at the annual classic and the last time I would set foot on the glorious Comiskey diamond. It would also be the last time I would see Martin. Stealing a few moments to catch up, I told him about the umpire schools I'd been trying to get into for several years. Each attempt was met with failure due to the color of my skin. Martin listened thoughtfully, then advised me with words I took to heart: "Motley, don't give up. Times have changed. They're going to have to open their doors sooner or later. And if you ever need me, you know where to find me."

His words meant the world to me, renewing my determination as I continued applying to all of the umpire schools in existence. Turns out that Dr. Martin was indeed right: in January of 1957, I successfully got entrée into the prestigious Al Somers Umpire School in Daytona Beach, Florida, becoming one of that school's first black students.

When I heard that Martin would not be returning to head the Negro League in the spring of 1957, I decided it was time for me to bow out as well. I figured without his leadership the league would lose even more of its luster, since he was the last of the Negro League old guard. And at any rate, I was ready to move on to my next adventure, whatever that might be. Although I had officially moved on, I did umpire a few Monarchs home games on and off throughout the 1957 and '58 seasons, helping out when needed and able, although I was no longer living the life of a "road baller."

My swan song to a league that had made my dreams come true was a bittersweet one. At age 35, I was one of the Negro Leagues' longest-reigning umpires, having served a full decade in its 40-year history. Thanks to my time in the Negro Leagues, I had developed a unique personal style, learned and developed a craft, and stood on the diamond with some of the most incredible black athletes of the Twentieth century. But like all good things, my time in black baseball had come to an end. In my heart of hearts, I knew it was time to move on. I was only hopeful that I could make the jump like Jackie Robinson and become the first black umpire in the majors. I knew I had what it took, and I was well on my way.

12
GOING BACK TO SCHOOL

"You may encounter defeats, but you must not be defeated!"
* Maya Angelou *

FOR YEARS I HAD BEEN TRYING to get accepted into umpire school. I had gotten close several times, but in each instance, once the powers-that-be found out I was black, the door was slammed in my face. Unfortunately, without entrance into umpire school, my dreams of umping in the majors would go unrealized. Since the field of umpiring was becoming more and more competitive, umpire school was made a prerequisite for placement into any organized league. All league presidents in "organized baseball" were looking for trained umpires, ones they felt had the most training and knowledge of how to handle all game situations. I felt like I had those credentials, but like all the other umpires in the Negro American League, I had never been to an umpire school. In Kansas City there was a local umpire association that met monthly to stay abreast of current issues and rules, and for a time I was the only black member of that group. Despite this obvious plea for acceptance on my behalf, I couldn't find a single school willing to take me.

Bill McGowan, a veteran major league umpire who had umpired in the American League for nearly 30 years, ran one of the most prestigious umpire schools in the country. Located in Rockledge, Florida, the school had been in operation since 1940 and had placed countless graduates into the major and minor leagues. As early as 1949 I began calling and writing McGowan seeking an opportunity to attend his school. I was sure that my professional experience in the Negro Leagues as well as my Ban Johnson League participation made me far more qualified than most other candidates. After briefly speaking with McGowan on the phone and mailing in my application, he informed me that he would be in touch with me via mail. In a letter dated January 16, 1950, he informed me, "Your age, weight, and height are excellent. We will be glad to enroll you for our second class, which starts on February 11, 1950." I was elated!

After receiving my acceptance letter, I called McGowan again to get more detailed information, since time was of the essence and I had less than a month to arrange my transportation to Florida. As I spoke with him on the phone, I noticed that McGowan sounded more distant than in our previous conversation. Sure enough, as the conversation turned he made his point, which hit me like a cold slap in the face: "I've reexamined your application and noticed your experience umpiring in the Negro Leagues. I need to know something very important. Are you a colored boy?" Blindsided by his question, I got a sinking feeling in the pit of my stomach. "Yes sir," I tentatively replied. The tone in his voice became suddenly somber. Coldly, he continued as he stuttered over his words: "In ten years of running this school I have never been faced with this situation. You are the first colored boy who has ever applied to this school. We have a law here in the state of Florida, which basically says that 'whites can't teach blacks and blacks can't teach whites.' Therefore, by order of state law I'm going to have to rescind my invitation to you." I was devastated.

McGowan is one of the few umpires inducted into the Baseball Hall of Fame at Cooperstown. I'm sure his admission was based on his trendsetting colorful manner of umpiring and his impressive record of dedicated service, which includes an astonishing 2,541 consecutive games. It certainly wasn't based on his lack of Branch Rickey-like efforts to integrate his umpire school. That much I can attest to.

Drawing hope from Dr. Martin's words—that the walls of segregation would eventually tumble down—I tried McGowan's and every other umpire school in the country every year from that point forward. The answer was always the same, "No!" I would either be informed directly, "no coloreds allowed," or after accepting me and discovering I was black I would be told a lame excuse like, "Oh we're sorry, we didn't realize we were at capacity." I heard more bullshit excuses over those seven years than I care to remember. The denials always came over the telephone. Not one of those schools ever had the nerve to put their rejections in writing.

All I wanted was an opportunity. I was willing to start at the lowest level if necessary, because I knew I could work my way up. But after having the door slammed in my face on so many occasions, I decided to try to sidestep the umpire school altogether. I got my hands on a media guidebook that contained the names and address of baseball league presidents in every class of baseball, and I wrote each president a handwritten letter in an effort to receive consideration for each league. In return, I either received a letter of denial or no reply at all. My efforts seemed futile until Frank Shaughnessy, the president of the International League, agreed to a meeting in 1954. Deciding to make it a working vacation, I used the Shaughnessy meeting as a means to treat my bride of a year to a belated honeymoon trip. My wife and I drove from Kansas City to Buffalo, New York, where I had scheduled an 8 a.m. meeting with Mr. Shaughnessy at his office. I was received graciously, although I could tell from his initial expression that Mr. Shaughnessy was taken aback that I was a Negro. Our meeting lasted for a good half hour as we discussed my experiences, desires, and goals. At the conclusion of the meeting he lowered the boom: "We don't have an opening right now, *but* if something comes up we will certainly consider you." Before I could respond, Shaughnessy cut me off: "Now I know you've probably heard this all before and I can't help but think it might not mean much to you, and I wouldn't blame you for thinking my words were an empty promise." My hope flickered to life. *Was this guy for real?* I wondered. He shook my hand and looked me right in the eyes, continuing, "Bob Motley, you *will* hear from me." Well, I'm here to tell you, I ain't heard from him yet!

Shortly after my meeting with Shaughnessy, Bill McGowan passed away. Al Somers, another veteran umpire whose career had been contained to Triple-A minor league baseball, took over the reins of the school and changed the name to the Al Somers Umpire School of Daytona Beach, Florida. After receiving another denial in 1955, I pulled out all the stops in 1956. In addition to my own letter and application, I reached out to Dr. Martin and asked for his assistance in helping me to get accepted into Somers' school. Without hesitation, he obliged, writing the following letter on my behalf:

December 18, 1956

Dear Al,

I am writing you in reference to umpire Robert Motley, 1600 West 37th Street, Kansas City, Missouri, who has umpired for the Negro American Baseball League for several years.

We have had many umpires in our league and in my opinion I think he is one of the best we have had. He is now seeking a position as umpire in organized baseball and I certainly hope he will be successful because I think he is well qualified.

Any consideration you give him will be deeply appreciated by our league and myself.

Very truly yours,

J. B. Martin
President, Negro American League

This time, everything fell right into place. Al Somers called me personally in January 1957 to welcome me to the school. He was very upfront, letting me know that I might face some "resistance" from some of my classmates, but he promised that he would personally do everything within his power to make sure I was well taken care of and comfortable. I had to pinch myself—my persistence had finally paid off. After seven years of trying to gain acceptance, I was now on my way. My wife, ever supportive, was just as excited about my opportunity. Within a few weeks of accepting my invitation during a blistery Missouri winter, I packed my bags into my 1951 Buick Sedan and headed off to the Sunshine State. Determined to get there as quickly as possible, I made the 1,200-mile drive by myself in less than 24 hours, stopping only for gas. Needless to say, when I arrived in Daytona Beach I was exhausted.

The journey had been relatively easy and stress free until about halfway through the drive when I reached the heart of the South. Echoes of my childhood flashed in my mind. In the late 1950s, a black man driving through the South by himself was a marked man. I kept my foot on the gas and slowed down for nothing. But as fate would have it, I was forced to slow down once I reached the city limits of Meridian, Mississippi, as I got caught up in traffic following a basketball game. I kept my eyes on the road, avoiding eye contact with the hundreds of cars rumbling around me, all filled with white passengers. A car full of five or six young college-aged boys pulled up behind me and started honking their horn, beckoning for me to pull off to the side of the road. My heart racing, palms sweating, body trembling, I reached over and pulled my trusty facemask into my lap; it had served as protection numerous times before—I just hoped this wouldn't have to be one such time. All the while I kept my eyes fixed forward, despite the honking and taunting jeers from those boys behind me. Nervously, I made my slow trek through the bumper-to-bumper traffic, constantly glancing into the rear-view mirror to make sure that those idiots hadn't jumped out of their car to storm mine.

As the traffic began to ease up, I could see a clearing about a half mile away. At this point the boys had pulled up beside me. Scared out of my wits, I devised a plan to trick them into thinking I had a car full of sleeping Negroes with me. I rolled down my window so that they could hear my voice. Before they could say something to me, I shouted as loudly as possible, "Hey Jim, Bill, Bob—wake up! These guys want us to pull over to the side of the road!" I heard one of the boys say, "Oh shit!" Just then they hit their brakes and the road opened up before me. I floored it, going as fast as that ol' Buick would take me. I got the hell out of Meridian, and never drove back through that town again.

I FINALLY ARRIVED AT the Al Somers Umpire School around ten o'clock at night, relieved to have made it in one piece and exhausted from the trip. I made my way to the front desk of the housing facilities to register. Manning the check-in desk was an old cantankerous white man thumbing through a well-worn newspaper. I politely introduced myself and told him I was reporting for umpire school. Looking up from his paper he grunted when he saw me. Snatching a key from the wall, he barked, "Here you go, boy. Your room is down at the end of the hall." He threw my room key at me, then lowered his head and immediately went back to thumbing through his newspaper. I thought to myself, *What the hell have I gotten myself into?*

Once inside my room, I began to get very nervous—probably paranoid after driving all day and encountering a hint of violence. Had Al Somers lured me to Florida to have me lynched? I wanted to call my wife to let her know I had arrived safely, but I was too afraid to leave the room. Shaking with fear, I moved both the credenza and chest of drawers up against the door, which I bolted shut. As I had done back on those Negro League bus rides and on my drive down, I kept my trusty facemask nearby as I turned off the light and tried to get some rest.

After sleeping all night with one eye open, I awoke and anxiously made my way onto the school's grounds. My only purpose was to meet Al Somers as quickly as possible. I had made up my mind that if I got that same strange vibe from him that I had received at check in, then I was going to get in my car and head home. Damn that $118 course fee—these crackers weren't going to tar and feather me. But all my fears quickly vanished upon meeting Somers, who greeted me with open arms. As promised, he and the rest of his staff made me feel right at home. I immediately dismissed the apprehension I had felt upon my arrival. (Surprisingly enough, in the ensuing weeks that old night watchman and I became quite friendly with each other.)

Al Somers was a tall, broad-shouldered, balding man who had earned the reputation of the finest umpire instructor of his time. A class act, he was also one of the gentlest, kindest men I have ever met. A no-nonsense teacher who knew the rules like the back of his hand, we often referred to him as "The Whip" because he knew just how to whip us into shape. Al was firm, but he genuinely cared about his pupils.

His school, located where the Daytona 500 Speedway now stands, was everything it promised to be. The intense six-week training course consisted of a rigorous six-days-a-week schedule that began at 10 o'clock in the morning and didn't conclude until 10 o'clock at night. In the morning we did some calisthenics and went through a series of classes; then at 3 p.m. we were given a four-hour break to relax, eat dinner, and socialize. At 7 p.m. we reconvened for night classes. We were taught every nuance of the official rules; the proper stance, voice control, and ball and strike procedure of the home plate umpire; the proper position of the body for calling field plays; the proper positions of the two-, three-, and four-men systems; and the proper appearance and conduct we were to adhere to both on and off the field. Even with all the experience I had umpiring in the Negro Leagues, once I immersed myself in my studies, I realized just how little I actually knew about the craft. My trusty rulebook and my amateur and Negro League game experiences had all given me the basics, but umpire school was about fine-tuning my abilities and shaping me into a more skilled arbiter.

Attending umpire school was one of the greatest thrills of my life. I'll never forget the first day of class, stepping onto the field with all of the new enrollees—72 whites and two blacks. The other black student, Clift Mathews from Washington, D.C., and I were basically the Jackie Robinson and Larry Doby of umpires-in-training. Since I was entering into a world where no black man had ever gone, I made up my mind right then and there to give it my best shot.

Of course, the best training couldn't exist without a qualified staff. Al's assistants included several professional-level umpires including Lou DiMuro, who would go on to become an outstanding major league arbiter. At different points during the six-week session we also received instructions from special guests, including major league umpires Ed Rommel, John Flaherty, Ed Hurley, and John Rice; and Hall of Fame greats Tris Speaker and Hank Greenberg.

My on-field training was mentally and physically intense, but also fun. What made it even more enjoyable for me was that I didn't sense any prejudicial feelings from any of my classmates. Even the Southerners didn't behave like the typical Southerners I had grown up around. Everyone was there to learn and have a good time while doing so. For field training, we always broke up into two teams and played about three to four innings of baseball, setting up situations to demonstrate different play scenarios. An instructor was stationed at each base to provide guidance as needed. I looked forward to these daily sessions on the diamond. There we could develop our own technique, get one-on-one instructions and critiques, and check out the skills of our fellow students.

Not to be braggadocios, but as far as style and pizzazz were concerned, I was far ahead of the rest. I think most of those men equated professional umpiring with strictness in tone and manner. It's like their minds wouldn't allow their bodies to let loose. Of course, my training in the Negro Leagues, which had allowed me complete freedom to do my own thing, played a big part in giving me this edge. By the end of week one I had endeared myself to Somers. He loved my energy and enthusiasm and was very high on me. He and his instructors always praised my work ethic and were diligent in their efforts to help me strengthen my weak areas as well.

My toughest competitor was another student by the name of Al Salerno. Salerno and I were in a neck-and-neck race for top honors in our class. He was smart, enthusiastic, personable, experienced, and extremely focused on learning every nuance about umpiring. Immediately upon graduation, Salerno went into the minor league system and by 1961 had made it to the top—the American League.

After working there for seven years and becoming one of the finest mediators in U.S. sports, Salerno and fellow umpire Bill Valentine were fired for trying to organize a union for umpires. He and Valentine sued, but unfortunately a New York federal court ruled against them due to the fact that baseball was exempt from antitrust laws. Sadly, in my opinion, the majors let go of one of their best officials in the process.

Tests were given each week, and at the end of the six-week training a final exam consisting of both a written and on-field part was administered to determine each student's overall grade. The written exam consisted of 160 questions dealing with every rule imaginable, while the on-field final involved calling plays at different bases as well as calling balls and strikes. I aced the written portion of the exam and received some of the highest marks for the on-field portion as well. I graduated sharing top honors of my class with Salerno, Richard DeChaine, and Harold Wymers.

Upon graduation, the new graduates found out where their first professional assignment would be. The instructors—who had ties to every amateur, college, minor, and major league system—had been putting feelers out for weeks trying to place their best candidates, so it was often the case that those who graduated at or near the top of their class were assured placement. As a matter of fact, George Trautman, president of the National Association of Professional Baseball Leagues had his underlings Hal Weafer and Jim Tobin on hand to scout us young hopefuls. From the graduating class the year before me, Al had placed 31 men in various leagues from Class D teams to the Triple-A.

Being one of the tops in my class meant I was a shoo-in for a job. Except for one small problem: the color of my skin. On graduation day, Al called me into his office. With tears in his eyes he told me bluntly, "Bob Motley, I have tried my best to place you somewhere. But no general manager in Triple-A, Double-A, Single-A, or B ball seems to have an opening for a black umpire. I am so sorry to have to tell you that. But Bob, I'm going to keep on working until I can get you placed somewhere, because you are the best here and you should be working. Now, you go on home and we will give you a call when we find something for you."

I was dumbstruck and frustrated. What was I going to tell my wife? After I had performed the best and worked so hard, how could I be denied an employment opportunity? As many of my white counterparts were heading off to various assignments around the country, their valedictorian was packing his bags and preparing to make the long drive home. My wife received me with the support and loving encouragement I had grown accustomed to from her. I tried my best not to let on how devastated I was. I did not want to burden my lady and my little girl with my loss. But Pearline knew, and her undying optimism helped me survive a very difficult and emotional period in my life.

I settled back into my regular work routine at General Motors, yet every time the phone rang at home I ran to it thinking Al was calling with some good news. Three months went by without a single word from Al. Finally in June I called him. He started in with that "I'm sorry" tone in his voice, and began the same spiel: "Bob, I'm still trying to place you somewhere but I'm having no luck. Nobody wants a black umpire." For weeks the words "nobody wants a black umpire" rang in my head. At the end of the baseball season I called him again, but his answer was the same. Disappointed but undaunted, I asked him if I could return the following year to take the advanced course. Not wanting to miss out on the $118 tuition fee, Al replied without hesitation, "You know we'd be glad to have you."

In January 1958, I again loaded my suitcase into my Buick and headed back to Daytona Beach. I came to school more determined than ever to be the best. In addition to me, three new black students had joined the brigade—Henry Johnson, Grover Carr, and Aaron

Middlebrooks. Mathews, the other black candidate from the previous year, had faded into obscurity.

Johnson and Carr had come to school together from the Detroit, Michigan area. They had never been to the Deep South and didn't quite understand the seriousness of "colored folks knowing their place." One Sunday afternoon on our day off from training, the three of us went into town to have a look around. Upon entering the local five-and-dime store, the first thing they noticed were drinking fountains labeled "white" and "colored." They stood there momentarily, stunned and growing obviously incensed. I thought to myself, *These Negroes are gonna get my black behind lynched for sure.* Sensing how angry they were, I grabbed them both, pleading with them, "Let's get out of here before we get thrown under the jail." They wouldn't leave quietly, resisting me so much that the three of us nearly broke into a fight right there in the store. It took some doing, but I was finally able to coax them back into my car. The whole way back to the training facility, they bitched, moaned, and threatened to go back and take care of their unfinished business—namely ripping that sign down and taking the drinking fountain with it. You can bet I never went into town with them again.

Middlebrooks, the third student, was the oddest man I've ever met in my life. First of all, *each and every day* during our four-hour break, he would get dressed up in a suit and tie, go into town, and visit funeral homes to see who had died. His obsession with death was downright bizarre. I don't know what he did when he got to each funeral home, but the fact that he made it a daily routine was way too weird for me. He invited me several times to go with him, but I always politely declined. One day when I had finally had it with the invitations I snapped: "Man, stop asking me to go to those damn funerals. I don't wanna have nothing to do with them dead folks!" He finally stopped inviting me, although he would still report back to me his findings: "Mr. Smith died. He made such a beautiful, peaceful-looking corpse."

Apparently, having a few screws loose was not a strike against a potential umpire, even if he was a lackluster one at that. More evidence of Middlebrooks' nuttiness came in the tens of pictures of his dog that he carried around in his wallet. Wooly was a three-legged, medium-sized hound that Middlebrooks always referred to as his "baby." Now, I've seen people who are crazy about their dogs and treat them like family, but this guy went a little too far. Middlebrooks talked about Wooly in such a loving and longing manner that we all came to the consensus that he had an "unnatural" relationship with his mutt.

My 1958 class redeemed itself with two white students whose names would eventually become synonymous with sports and baseball. Brent Musburger, who first worked in the Midwest League as an umpire in 1959, later turned his talents in another direction by becoming a renowned sports analyst on television. During our time together at umpire school, Brent showed himself to be extremely outgoing and personable. What I remember most about him was that he seemed more interested in talking about the game than actually being out on the field partaking in the action. Of course, that ultimately proved true when he found his calling in broadcasting, where he has enjoyed an illustrious career.

The other student who would go on to gain some notoriety was Bruce Froemming. Barely out of high school, Bruce was a hustler who had a great enthusiasm for learning. Always inquisitive, Froemming seemed to ask the "stupid questions" that everyone else wanted to know but were too embarrassed to ask. His eagerness led him to become the youngest umpire to ever gain acceptance into the Pacific Coast League at the tender age of 18. After roughly 13 years in the minors he finally worked his way up to the National League in 1971. Today, Froemming is still going strong as baseball's most senior crew chief. However, his recent anti-Semitic remarks about an umpire administrator have tarnished his stellar reputation as one of the league's most respected arbiters. Controversial or not, his long 30-plus years in the bigs is enviable.

When exam time rolled around, again I was the only student to answer all the questions correctly, and was number one on field exercises as well. After graduating for the second year in a row at the top—this time at the "advanced" level—I felt more confident that I would earn an assignment somewhere. On graduation day, Somers again called me into his office and gave me the same ol' rigmarole. "Motley, things *will* break for you sometime. Now, you go on home. . . ." *Yeah, yeah, yeah—I've heard that before*, my mind shouted. I just sat there, weary with disappointment and sick down deep inside. It became quite clear to me that no matter how good an umpire I was, my skin color would prevent me from ever being a part of the "good ol' boys network." The elite network of umpire dons who had readily accepted my underlings would certainly see to that.

My emotions had gone past the point of frustration. I felt cheated and disillusioned. Fortunately, my wife and daughter had come down for the graduation ceremony as a show of support, so having them there helped soften the discriminatory blow. Still, as I drove off the grounds of the Al Somers Umpire School for the last time, I felt as if every white person in the country had it in for me. For the first time in my life I was mad at America. I thought about my forefathers who had battled slavery and my own father who had possibly been murdered by hatemongers. I thought about my mother who had toiled daily for wealthy white families for a mere pittance that barely supported her family. Then I thought about my own six-year-old daughter and wondered what type of future she would have in a country that still could not fully embrace all of its citizens. I had had it!

LOOKING FOR A WAY OUT and needing time to clear my raging disgust for a country that I had put my life on the line for in World War II, I decided to accept an offer from one of my umpire school buddies who suggested that my family and I come visit him in his hometown of Havana, Cuba. Carlos Alejandro Sanchez was one of two Cuban students in the class of '58 with hopes of being the first Latino to break into the lily-white umpiring world of organized baseball in America. Sympathizing with my situation, Sanchez invited me to visit his country so that I could experience for myself what he called "the graciousness of the island and its people." He also suggested that it would be an opportunity for me to investigate the possibility of umpiring in Cuba, just in case "America doesn't get its act together and let you umpire."

Back then, Cuba was a playground for Americans. A hot spot with legalized gambling, a festive nightlife, pristine beaches, scrumptious cuisine, world-renowned art galleries, and rhythmic Afro-Latin flavored music, Cuba was hailed "the jewel of the Caribbean." On long bus rides, I had overheard Negro League players talk about their incredible experiences playing winter ball on the island. Cuba sounded like the sort of magical paradise that might do a worn-down man like me some good. What was most intriguing was the fact that all the players had said that in Cuba, a black man could just be a man and not have to worry about paying the social consequences for it. It sounded about perfect to me.

Immediately after graduation, my family and I drove to Key West, Florida, bought our $10 round-trip airplane tickets, hopped on a puddle jumper, and took the 30-minute plane ride 90 miles across the Atlantic Ocean to Havana. Sanchez met us at the airport, took us to our hotel, and gave us a whirlwind tour of the city. My wife and I had never been any place as exotic and beautiful as Cuba in our lives. The salacious nightlife, rich Cuban customs, and beautiful and friendly people of Havana enthralled us. Our taste buds were awoken with plantains, yucca, malanga, and grouper, as well as fresh bananas, oranges, papaya, and mangos. I've never been much of a drinker or smoker, but as the old saying goes, "when in Rome, do as the Romans do." So I enjoyed Mojitos and puffed on Montecristo Cuban cigars. At one minute past midnight every night, we watched a parade of musicians and dancers prance through the streets of Old Havana. The festive Cuban people really knew how to live, and the atmosphere is exactly what my weary soul required.

As promised, Sanchez introduced me to a few of the bigwigs in the Cuban baseball world. One Cuban baseball dignitary told me that I had an open invitation to come back to Cuba to umpire any time I wanted. Since the weather allowed them to play baseball year round, I made plans to take advantage of the offer in the near future. In the week we spent on the island, my wife and I even began looking at apartments that we could rent upon our return.

To give me a taste of umpiring in Cuba, Sanchez arranged for me to umpire a non-league exhibition game at Havana's famed "El Gran Estadio del Cerro," or El Cerro Stadium, as it was known in pre-revolution Cuba. El Cerro was a recently built, spacious, 55,000-seat pitchers' ballpark boasting a major league quality playing field. At the time, it was considered the grandest state-of-the-art baseball park in all of Latin America. It was quite the impressive venue to make my Cuban debut.

Umpiring in Cuba was no different than umpiring in America, since the signs for safe and out are the same in any language. But my experience was anything but the norm I had become accustomed to in America. The Cuban fans gave me an incredibly warm reception beyond anything I had ever experienced in the States. The Cubans loved my outrageous flair. I assumed they had never seen an umpire perform the gymnastic-type stunts I was pulling on the field. I ate up their cheers and let myself go, becoming ever more the showman. My colorful style was right in step with the players' spirited play. Just from that one little game, Sanchez told me he overheard Cuban fans referring to me as "el Negro loco," or "crazy black man." I didn't know if it was a compliment or not, but Sanchez assured me that the Cubans had enjoyed my style. After the game, several fans asked for my autograph, a first for me. I nudged my wife and said, "Honey, I could get used to this."

By the time we made it home to Kansas City, I had still received no communication from Somers. So, I began my next plan of attack: I would return to Cuba where my talents were wanted. Just weeks away from solidifying my plans to go back to the island, the call I had been waiting for over the past year and a half finally came. We were in the middle of dinner, so oddly enough this was the one time I did not run to pick up the telephone. When I least expected it, I received my first offer from Al: the Pacific Coast League had a contract in the works. So much for returning to the isle of Cuba; I was headed west.

13
TAKING AIM
ON THE MAJORS

"The Coast League was, in fact, the third major league."
* Eddie Basinski, minor league veteran *

LESS THAN EIGHT MONTHS AFTER our visit to Cuba, a new government spearheaded by the charismatic and powerful Fidel Castro led a historic revolution, overthrowing dictator Fulgencio Batista. Castro promised sweeping social reforms and a new, democratic, and corruption-free Cuba. Soon after establishing power, however, Castro aligned his administration with the Communist doctrine and ultimately banned all international sports relations, especially with America. I was fortunate enough to be cradled in the arms of America's shore instead of being caught in the middle of Cuba's changing political regime, but unfortunately Castro's indignation for America would keep me from ever returning to the island to umpire.

If you have a little faith, things often go the way they are supposed to, proving that life has a way of working itself out, as I say, for the best and better. My week in Cuba had cured me of my recent anger toward my country, and I was ready to get back into the swing of life. To that end, Al Somers' phone call in August of 1958 came right on time. Al was umpiring in the Pacific Coast League, but his season was cut short by a broken arm that would require surgery and keep him out for the remainder of the season. Al's misfortune became my good fortune, because he insisted to the powers-that-be that I be his replacement. Even though I was being called up toward the end of the '58 season for just a couple weeks of assignments, I was thrilled beyond belief.

Of course I called everybody I knew to tell them of my great opportunity. I even phoned Dr. Martin and thanked him for his encouragement through the years. Always a class act, he offered in turn to compose two letters on my behalf: one to the Pacific Coast League president, Leslie O'Connor; and another for me to hand directly to my crew chief upon arrival at my first assignment. The letters would both thank them for giving me the opportunity, and ask them to look out for me.

It was very seldom that someone from umpire school was sent directly to Triple-A ball. Usually, former students were sent to lower-class affiliations to continue to hone their crafts. Al Somers had stuck to his word, telling me that he would not insult me by putting me into the lower classes of ball, so I was indeed honored. I was a rarity, and now just one step away from the majors.

I had big shoes to fill, stepping in as a replacement for Al. I knew everyone would be checking out this new kid on the block for two reasons: my skin color and my worthiness of filling in for the legendary Somers. Once in the league, I was reminded frequently what a good umpire Al had been and how dedicated he was to his craft and the Pacific Coast League (PCL). Even though he was known to be fiery and often got into arguments on the field, he was well respected. My fellow umpires also talked about how he always dressed "neat as a pin."

During this period, Triple-A baseball had three league affiliations: the American Association, which consisted of Midwest teams; the International League, which hosted teams in the East; and the Pacific Coast League, comprised of the western teams. Each league had eight teams, and just like nowadays, each team was a farm affiliate of a major league organization. Of the three leagues, the PCL was the most prestigious. With no major league team west of St. Louis before 1958, the PCL was *the* premier regional baseball league of its time. Many considered it the "major leagues of the west."

The PCL carried so much weight in baseball that there was some consideration given to it becoming a third major league. In the early 1950s it was even upgraded in its classification to an "open" league, placing it a "step above the Triple-A level." In all honesty, all they had to do was add 10,000 to 15,000 seats in any of the stadiums, doll them up a bit, and they could have been major league-caliber ballparks. In the years before Seattle had their Mariners or Los Angeles, San Francisco, San Diego, or Phoenix had their major league clubs, each of those cities, at one time or another, had its own brand of high-quality baseball that helped comprise the teams of the PCL. Once the Giants and Dodgers moved westward in 1958, however, it sealed the fate for any of the minor league affiliates moving up to big-league status. During my tenure, the teams comprising the PCL were the Vancouver Mounties, Phoenix Giants, Portland Beavers, Spokane Indians, San Diego Padres, Salt Lake City Bees, Seattle Rainiers, and the Sacramento Solons. Most of those franchises now have either disbanded or integrated into other organizations. Similar to the Negro Leagues, franchises in the PCL throughout its history went through plenty of change, switching names, cities, and ownership.

The PCL crowds weren't nearly as raucous as they had been in the Negro Leagues. A typical minor league park held about 20,000 people, but was rarely, if ever, filled to capacity. Frankly I didn't care if they held only 20 people and were *never* filled, so long as I was allowed to umpire; I was as close to realizing my ultimate dream as I had ever been.

Strangely enough, I almost didn't make it to my first PCL assignment. Fate debated playing a cruel trick on me. The league office had routed my flight from Kansas City through San Francisco in order for me to meet up with the other members of my umpire crew so that we would arrive together in Phoenix, where my first game was scheduled. Meeting my new associates—Carl "Cece" Carlucci, Al Maxey, and Bob St. Clair—was exciting and nerve-racking at the same time. Outside of umpire school and Ban Johnson League games, this would be the first time I'd ever umpired with a "professional" white crew. I didn't anticipate any problems, but then again, I didn't know what to expect.

I really should not have been concerned with racial issues at all, for once we had boarded the plane and were en route to Phoenix, we had bigger problems on our hands. The pilot abruptly announced that our flight was making an emergency landing due to a bomb threat. Everyone was tense as we made a nail-biting, nose-first landing in Bakersfield, California. When the plane hit the runway, it literally bounced along like a basketball until the pilot was able to bring the prop job to a screeching halt. It scared us all to death. Compounding our fear was the fact that police cars and fire trucks surrounded our plane on the tarmac. The passengers stopped screaming long enough to scamper off the plane so that detectives and bomb-sniffing dogs could do their work. Thankfully, no bomb was found, and within a couple hours we were airborne once again. I should have known that as painstaking as my journey to the PCL had been, making it to my first game wouldn't be easy, either.

Upon our safe landing in Phoenix, the umpire crew was met by an escort who shuttled us directly to the stadium. Remarkably, we arrived only a few minutes late, and the start of the game was only delayed ten minutes. As I hurried into my umpire uniform and scurried through the runway that led out onto the PCL stage, I didn't have any opportunity to take in the overwhelming magnitude of the moment. Here I was about to umpire my first minor league game, and I was just glad to be alive!

Before leaving Kansas City I had purchased brand-new umpiring gear and a suit from the All American Sports Supply Company, which gave special discounts to Al Somers graduates. My navy blue wool uniform, athletic supporter, two caps, two pairs of shoes, facemask, "balloon" or "blow up" breast protector, leg guards, and travel case all cost me under $200. I may have still been shaking slightly from the horrifying flight, but I sure as heck looked sharp as a tack in my new duds.

I made my organized baseball-umpiring debut on Monday, August 18, 1958. As the Phoenix Giants began a three-game series against the Spokane Indians at Municipal Stadium, I took to the field with my new crew of minor league veterans: Carlucci at home plate; St. Clair at first base; and Maxey at second. Taking my spot at third base, I became the Larry Doby of the Pacific Coast League—its second black umpire. Immediately after the game I handed Carlucci the letter I had received from Dr. Martin. He got a big kick out of the gesture and talked to me at length about the one other black umpire who had been in the Pacific Coast League since 1954, Emmett Ashford. I quickly felt at ease with Carlucci, as he was engaging, light-hearted, and personable.

The next day I met with league president Leslie O'Connor, who had briefly served as Major League Baseball's interim commissioner after Kennesaw Mountain Landis' death in 1944. At his office, I signed my contract for a whopping $500 a month. If I was retained for a second year, then my salary would increase to $750 a month! Before leaving his office, O'Connor reached into his pocket and pulled out a crisp $100 bill and told me to go out and have a nice meal on him. I knew right away that the PCL was definitely a first-class organization, and that I was in good hands.

My first series in Phoenix was exciting, although I did get off to somewhat of a rocky start. In the third game, on a 2-2 count, Giants batter Andre Rogers checked his swing on a pitch that was high and inside. From my vantage point it looked as if his bat broke the surface of the plate. When Carlucci, the home plate umpire, did not signal the call, and looked toward me for my assessment, I called it a strike. Phoenix Giants manager Red Davis stormed out of the dugout demanding the call be consulted with St. Clair at first. St. Clair overruled me, stating he thought Rogers had checked his swing. Not disputing my fellow ump, I rescinded my call and agreed with St. Clair's call. That only escalated the problem, because then an irate Bobby Bragan, Spokane's manager, came running out of his dugout. After a heated conference that took place at home plate, Carlucci ruled the call was indeed a check swing, filling up the count at 3-2. Bragan, incensed, played the rest of the game under protest. The next day, the dispute was written up in the sports section of *The Phoenix Gazette* newspaper. As it turned out, the Indians eked out a 7-4 victory over the Giants, and I learned an important lesson that day: Always go with your gut and *never* back down from your initial call.

In the PCL it was standard to work with a three-man crew. When breaking a new umpire in, however, four umpires were used during the rookie's first few games. Initially I was assigned to work with Carlucci and St. Clair, but then I began to switch every five days or so with other crews. Before the start of each game, every umpire was given specific tasks to perform. The third-base umpire was responsible for "rubbing down the balls." Dipping into a big bucket of dirt we called "Kentucky mud," the third-base ump would work the wet grit into six dozen brand-new game balls to take the shine off and curb their slickness. The groundskeeper would have the bucket in the umpires' dressing room ready for us at least two hours before game time. After the rub down, the bucket with the balls was given to the ball boy, who would in turn lock it up until game time so that no one could tamper with them. Meanwhile, the first-base umpire supervised the batting practice for each team. At a certain time, the head of the grounds crew would ring a bell, signaling the start and end times for each team. It was up to the umpire to make sure the teams switched off when they were supposed to, giving each their allotted time. The home plate umpire was given the luxury to relax in the dressing room, since he would be doing the bulk of the work during the game.

MY TWO FAVORITE PCL STADIUMS were Seattle's Sicks' Stadium and Los Angeles' Wrigley Field. Sicks' Stadium was a majestic stadium for a minor league ballpark. When the sky was crystal clear after a heavy rain, I could stand at home plate and see Mt. Rainier off in the distance, looming beyond the center-field wall. Wrigley Field mimicked Chicago's Wrigley with its beautiful green ivy growing along the right-field wall. It's a pity that both stadiums have since been demolished.

I was far more attached to stadiums than I ever was to ballplayers. Each stadium was a grand cathedral of sorts, in which I could rule over the land. A ballplayer was just a ballplayer. It may sound insensitive of me to place lesser value on the people instead of the place, but that's just how I felt. At the time, the players' names, positions, batting averages, and ERAs meant very little to me. I had "tunnel vision," and was intent on keeping my mind on my job. That meant I often appreciated the atmosphere more than the company. But in hindsight, I now realize that in my very first

PCL outing, I was in the presence of some formidable talent who were on their way to becoming major league greats: Maury Wills, Willie McCovey, and manager Bobby Bragan were all destined for the majors. Eventually, after I settled into the gig and began to notice players, I usually paid more attention to the black players, for obvious reasons. I'd occasionally give them the once over, assessing their skills and in my mind comparing them to the greats I had seen in the Negro Leagues. In addition to Wills and Hall of Famer McCovey, I was also impressed with Tommy Davis, Frank Howard, Willie Davis, and the "Dominican Dandy," future Hall of Famer Juan Marichal. A baby-faced hurler who had a lot of finesse and control on the mound, Marichal reminded me a lot of the great Cuban-born Negro League fireballer Luis Tiant Sr., whose son, Luis Tiant, became one of the greats of the game in the same era as Marichal. I remember thinking, *For a kid so young, Marichal certainly can make that ball hum.* Any one of those aforementioned standout black players of the PCL would have been stars in the Negro Leagues.

Whereas I noticed that the white players in the PCL were possibly more schooled in their approach to the game, these brothers, like the Negro Leaguers I had umpired, had a jazzier style on the field. Still, everyone had to tone things down in the PCL. Just as I had curtailed much of my flamboyant style, so too did many of the players I was now umpiring. They played a far less showy form of baseball than I had grown accustomed to, which helped to prove to the big-league club that they had the fundamentals to make it in the game, but made for a less entertaining day at the office for me.

I did see some good baseball in the PCL, but I have to honestly say that the level of play was only "as good" as the Negro Leagues had been in its declining years. It certainly wasn't any better. Considering the PCL was the top of the line of the minors, I expected to see a much higher caliber of play. While the PCL was dressed up with major league affiliations, quality stadiums, and first-rate travel accommodations, including plane rides and comfortable, air-conditioned buses, the quality of baseball wasn't what I had grown accustomed to in the Negro Leagues. The PCL had many talented players, but those players simply didn't seem to have as much heart and soul as the Negro Leaguers.

However, the PCL did have its advantages. Unlike the racism I encountered in my barnstorming Negro League days, the PCL exposed me to an environment of tolerance. Being on the west coast was wonderful. I could go where I wanted, when I wanted, without worry. If people in the West had prejudicial attitudes, they certainly did a better job of hiding them than where I had come from. I could stay in the same hotels as my white counterparts and walk down any street without wondering if I was in the "wrong part of town." After a game, I could even dine at restaurants with my white colleagues and no one would take a second glance. The one exception was the state of Utah, which still had concerns with the races mixing. So when in Salt Lake City I was forced to keep to myself.

The same general sense of tolerance carried over to the field of play. Similar to what I had seen during the Satchel Paige-Bob Feller All-Star's exhibitions, black and white players in the PCL seemed to be on one accord. Everyone wanted to win games and work diligently in the hopes of getting called up to the bigs. I don't think anyone wanted to risk doing or saying something stupid that could hinder an opportunity for advancement.

Still, that didn't stop players from looking for any edge possible—myself included. Setting my sights ever so high, I began to tell a little white lie that future Pro Football Hall of Famer Marion Motley was my first cousin. In 1946, one year before Jackie Robinson broke baseball's color barrier, Marion had smashed pro football's barrier. He was highly respected throughout the sporting community, and since people were assuming an association because of the last name, I went along with it. Even though we were more distantly related, I thought the connection might help bolster my efforts to move up the integration chain a little faster. In reality, it didn't seem to help my efforts at all, but it certainly provided an opportunity for me to get more press in newspapers than I might have otherwise.

All told, I spent two and one-third years in the PCL. I would have loved to have stayed longer, but the responsibilities of my primary role as a breadwinner and father began to supersede my dream of a big-league career. When I was but a kid working at the Jefferson Davis Hotel in Anniston, I had made a vow to myself that if I ever was blessed with a family like the well-dressed, intact, white families that frequented the lobby, I would do my absolute best to be a strong husband and father. Now with a second baby on the way, my concerns over the snail's pace in which the majors were embracing black umpires grew more and more pressing. In addition, it grew increasingly difficult for me to get time off from my full-time job at General Motors. I had been promoted several times to an upper-management level position that brought with it a substantial pay raise and great benefits. So I found myself at a crossroad. With baseball not offering me any real stability as far as my future was concerned, and only half a year's employment to boot, I chose job security and family happiness over my true passion and dreams. My own father, not by choice, was not able to be there for his children. I vowed to be there for mine.

Looking back, it was the right decision. Leaving the league was tough, but the memories that sustain me now are of spending time with my young children and wife. I have no regrets. I had the best of all worlds—a good, steady-paying job; an opportunity to continue umpiring in and around Kansas City; and the chance to be involved in the daily upbringing of my daughter and new baby boy, Byron. Best of all, I now had the PCL credit on my dossier, and felt that I could always return to the league in the future if I ever felt the need.

I COULD HAVE BEEN THE FIRST black umpire to make it to the majors, but I guess it wasn't meant to be. My chances were just as good as anybody else's, especially considering I was the minor leagues' second black umpire. I had all the qualities—experience, talent, and education (that important certificate from umpire school). But Major League Baseball worked on its own clock, as usual, when deciding when to open the door to a black man. I, like all black umpires of my time, was cognizant of the fact that many people in the upper echelons of baseball, and some players as well, would take issue with a black man being in charge on the diamond.

But by 1958, everyone in my circle of baseball friends was hopeful that the majors would soon ease up on its obvious exclusion of black umpires. Al Somers had assured me that several of his constituents in the inner circles of baseball had heard rumblings that the most qualified black umps were being considered and scouted. But, as it turns out, it was just more lip service being passed on down the chain. In truth it would take almost another decade before that door finally opened to a man who deservedly became the majors' first black umpire, Emmett Ashford.

Emmett was the absolute best umpire I ever umpired with, bar none. Not only was he a great arbiter, but he was also a showman extraordinaire. He had a style all his own and made no apologies for his outlandish techniques, energetic antics, and dapper manner of dress. Emmett was simply unique. I had known of Emmett's abilities since 1951, when he became the first black to umpire in the Southwest International League, a minor league. Keeping up with my competition, I read articles about his flamboyant style, which actually sounded a lot like mine, and I often wondered what it would be like to work with him. Furthermore, I figured if he could get into organized baseball, then certainly so could I.

During my first full year in the Pacific Coast League I finally had the opportunity to work with him. Initially, I thought Emmett might feel threatened by having a younger and equally experienced black umpire invade the territory he had held court at since 1954. After all, I had been to umpire school; he had not. I had umpired in the Negro Leagues for ten years; he had not. Surprisingly, Emmett immediately welcomed me into the fold and seemed happy to have me by his side. I found him to be a good-natured, funny man who took his work very seriously. We developed an immediate and friendly rapport, often referring to one another as "Jackie and Doby." We really had a good time together and rooted each other on.

I will never forget my first assignment with Emmett at Wrigley Field in Los Angeles. I was assigned to umpire first base, while Emmett took his turn behind the plate. As we walked out onto the field, he sauntered over behind home plate and laid down his mask, shin guards, and breast protector. I thought to myself, *What is he doing, stripping?* All of a sudden, he took off on a dead sprint toward center field. My gut reaction was one of nervousness, as I thought someone might be chasing him—or us. I almost started running, too. But as I watched his face I could see a wide toothy smile form and hear him chuckling to himself as he ran. I stood there watching this man, and I couldn't believe my eyes. When he got to the warning track, Emmett leaped through the air, ran up the center-field wall, turned a flip, landed on his feet, and then ran all the way back to the infield and slid into home plate. *The crowd went crazy!* I was flabbergasted. I thought to myself, *Now, here is an umpire!*

Needless to say, between the two of us, we gave fans quite a show that day. When we umpired the bases, it brought to my mind the awesome talent of the Banks and Baker double-play combination that I had grown so fond of during my days umpiring Monarchs games. A bang-bang double play turned successfully would get both of us airborne, exaggerating our calls to the delight of each other and the fans. We were quite a tandem, indeed. Emmett and I fed off of each other's energy and complemented each other's showmanship.

Being the only two black umpires in the league, sometimes our fellow white umps would say things to try to pit us against each other, attempting to get us to speak ill of one another. But like the Negro League ballplayers I had traveled with, Emmett and I had an unspoken bond of brotherhood between us, so their tactics fell short of ever causing any dissension between the two of us. Our competition was simply a friendly one.

When we would talk, the topic occasionally turned to us being the only two "spooks in the league," but it was always done in a joking manner, and we made a conscious effort not to belabor the point. It wasn't necessary to dwell on the obvious. Emmett told me about his experiences integrating the league, and about how some of the old-timers resented the fact that he had brought showmanship to the game. But as he said, "They got over it, and if they haven't they're gonna have to. I'm not here to please them." I admired his tenacity.

Emmett also told me that he had rarely faced any serious racial resistance during his tenure. Thankfully, neither did I in my time in the PCL. If we did encounter a hint of such behavior, we handled it with our sense of humor. The funniest incident that ever happened to me during my entire umpiring career actually occurred before a PCL game I umpired with Emmett. As Emmett, I, and a third (white) umpire walked onto the field, Emmett noticed the Portland Beavers manager (who shall remain nameless) glaring in our direction. At Emmett's prompting, I glanced over at the skipper, and sure enough the guy was throwing daggers at us with his stare.

Emmett jokingly said to me, "Motley, what'd you do to piss him off?"

"I ain't never even spoke to that man," I replied. "I don't know what his problem is."

Emmett again joked, "Humph, must be our Negroness!"

We laughed and proceeded to go to our respective positions. As I strolled down to third base, I heard the manager, still staring us down, mutter something under his breath. Usually I let this type of thing roll off my back, but on this day, probably because I was working with Emmett, I was feeling friskier. I casually remarked to the manager, "You're looking at Mr. Ashford and me like something's wrong. Did we do something to upset you?" Without batting an eye or cracking a smile he snapped, "No, I'm not mad at either one of you. It's those other two guys I'm mad at." With only three umpires on the field I was confused as to what "other two guys" he was talking about. I turned around to see whom he might be referring to, but since nobody else was in the vicinity I couldn't figure out for the life of me what he was talking about. He continued, "Uh-uh, ain't mad at the two of you. It's that goddamn Abraham Lincoln and Branch Rickey I'm mad at." Emmett and I laughed about that for years!

Knowing the majors were really in no hurry to take us in, neither Emmett nor I ever thought we'd see the red carpet rolled out for a black umpire, at least not as long as we were in the business. Boy, were we thankfully wrong. On April 11, 1966, in an American League game between the Cleveland Indians and the Washington Senators, my buddy Emmett Ashford, at 51 years of age, kicked the door down. It had been nearly 20 years since Jackie Robinson's breakthrough. Honestly it was a somewhat bittersweet moment for me, but I was still thrilled to death upon hearing the news of my friend's groundbreaking achievement. It was a well-deserved honor for a sensational umpire who had worked so hard over his career to achieve such an accomplishment. I sent Emmett a telegram and called to congratulate him.

Emmett shared many similar qualities to Jackie Robinson. He had grown up in integrated California, had some college education, and had been the first black to integrate the minor-league system— all qualities that in some ways outweighed my credentials. I had youth on my side, being almost ten years younger than Emmett, but his experience as well as the press he had garnered with the assistance of sports journalist Brad Pye Jr., spoke volumes. Also like Jackie, Emmett unfortunately paid a heavy price for his accomplishment, having to deal with taunts, threats, and name-calling. I'm honestly not so sure I would have handled such actions with as much grace as Emmett.

I was proud of Emmett for not compromising his exaggerated style when he reached "the show," even though he did tone it down a bit. I believe the fans would have loved his pregame ritual of running, flipping, and sliding into home plate, but the establishment would have never allowed it. No way they were going to encourage a black umpire to shine too much. However, the aspects of Emmett's inimitable style that remained brought a whole new image to the major league umpire that in my opinion has yet to be matched. Ron Luciano, another outrageous umpire famous for his behavior on the field, came close. But Emmett's style set the pace.

Emmett may have paved the way for other black umps, but the majors dragged its feet when it came to hiring another. It took seven years before Art Williams integrated the National League. Even now, some 40 years after Emmett's historic debut, there has only been a handful of African-American umpires in the majors. In a profession that pays upwards of $300,000 a year depending on seniority and responsibilities, there are currently only two African-Americans—

Chuck Meriwether and Kerwin Danley—out of a 68-man active major-league roster as of 2006, 60 years after Jackie Robinson's grand entrance.

Upon his retirement in 1970 after spending only four years in the major leagues, Emmett mentioned my name in interviews that ran in the national sports press on several occasions. I was honored that he mentioned me as one of the few Negro candidates he thought was qualified for a major-league umpire assignment. In 1972, I was further flattered upon running into Emmett and his wife Margaret at a Royals–A's game in Oakland, when he told me he had personally spoken to Major League Baseball commissioner Bowie Kuhn on my behalf, telling Kuhn that I should be selected as the next black umpire to be brought up to the majors. His support meant the world to me.

Emmett passed on in 1980. Those of us who appreciated his fortitude and uniqueness will forever admire his achievement of being the first black in his trade to make it to the top.

14

HANGING UP
THE TRUSTY FACEMASK

"Listen here, the world don't owe me nothing.
If anything, I owe the world!"
* Clifford "Connie" Johnson, Kansas City Monarchs *

AFTER LEAVING THE PACIFIC COAST LEAGUE I resumed my duties in Kansas City's Ban Johnson League, where I stayed until the mid-1970s. In addition to umpiring baseball, I also refereed high school and college basketball and football games, and coached men's and women's basketball, something I had done intermittently since 1947.

After I had hung up my facemask for good, I received phone calls from both the Umpires Association and the Major League Baseball commissioner's office. An impending umpire strike threatened to interrupt major league baseball in the late 1970s. The representatives wanted to know if, in the event of a strike, would I be willing to step in to umpire Royals home games in Kansas City? I gave the offer plenty of thought; after all, I was being offered the chance to fulfill my lifelong dream. But I declined for two reasons.

207

First, not that I'm a staunch unionist, but I didn't believe in crossing the picket line; and secondly, I didn't want to be referred to as a "scab" in a profession where I had devoted so much of my life's passion.

Several of my colleagues in the city thought I was crazy. They were chomping at the bit to work as subs, but my pride was more important than earning a few extra bucks as an "unofficial" major league umpire. Furthermore, this was undoubtedly not an entrée into the bigs, because once the strike was settled, I was sure all the temps would be back out on the street and the regulars would resume their positions. I wanted a permanent job, not a temporary handout. With no regret, I proudly stood by and still stand by my decision.

The final highlight of my umpiring career was participating in the 1973 College World Series at Omaha, Nebraska's Rosenblatt Stadium. Chosen as umpire-in-chief, I hired other officials from around the country to join me for the week-and-a-half-long tournament. The standout player from the series was the University of Minnesota's Dave Winfield.

Soon after the College World Series I retired permanently from umpiring. Although my heart was still very much in the game, I was in my 50s and felt it was time. I had been an active umpire for over half of my life, and had umpired in thousands of ballgames. It was hard to leave the game, but I didn't abandon my love of baseball completely. In 1973 I discovered a new passion, selling season tickets for the Kansas City Royals. The Royal Lancers is a unique organization that was founded by the Royals' original owner, Ewing Kauffman, whom we all fondly called "Mr. K." The Lancers is an incentive-based program in which local businessmen and women volunteer their time promoting the club by selling season tickets. I worked my butt off selling tickets, and in no time flat became the number-one season ticket salesman in the organization.

Although Lancers receive no pay, they do receive wonderful perks. My wife and I have traveled the world extensively on the Royals' dime. We also enjoy yearly trips to spring training, which we have done for over 30 years. As a bonus, because of my outstanding sales, I am one of three Lancers who has earned a personal parking space in front of Kauffman Stadium next to the Royals' current owner, David Glass. Yep, I've got it like that!

Today, I serve on the board of directors for the Negro Leagues Baseball Museum in Kansas City, a position I've held since the museum's inception in 1990. The museum is a proud reminder of the great legacy of a league that stood in the shadows of the majors for four decades. Every time I walk through the doors of the museum I feel a sense of overwhelming pride that wells up inside me. Never in my wildest dreams while traveling on those old rickety barnstorming buses, while staying in the homes of complete strangers, while leaping in the air as I called balls and strikes, or while watching Satchel's blistering fastballs smack the catcher's mitt, did I ever think there'd be a facility of this magnitude honoring the efforts of the men and women who made Negro baseball a thing to behold.

I am most proud of and honored by a display case in the museum that contains my umpire uniform, gear, and other artifacts from my collection of personal items. Located in the museum's centerpiece "The Field of Legends," alongside bronze statues of Hall of Famers Josh Gibson and Martin Dihigo, my time capsule is a flattering tribute that tickles me to death every time I see it.

Even now, all these years later, umpiring is still in my blood. And if I had my life to do over again, I would choose the exact same course. I may not have gotten to be "the first," but I am "the last"— *the last living umpire from the ol' historic Negro Baseball Leagues.* At times it seems like my days umpiring were several lifetimes ago. Yet they were only a few yesterdays ago. Many of the memories in my 80-plus-year-old mind are foggy at best, but the one thing that is indelibly clear to me is that I was a part of an incredible piece of Americana that jumpstarted the emergence of a race in the sporting world and beyond.

Unfortunately, many of the greatest legends of our league passed away long before the renaissance of interest in our league's history became en vogue. I think I can safely speak for the hundred or so still-living players when I say that as veterans of the leagues we never thought of ourselves as pioneers or legends. We were only doing what we loved to do—*playing the game of baseball.* The sands of time have labeled us as trailblazers, and so much more. And you know what? That's all right with me.

ACKNOWLEGMENTS

Our endless thanks to our wonderful family: Pearline Motley, Bobette Motley-Agee, Eugene Agee, Heather Roberta Brown, Stephanie Renee Brown, Chris Agee, Jason Agee, and Jeff Miiller. We greatly appreciate your encouragement, love, support, and enthusiasm for this book project.

We would also like to thank the following for their existence in our lives and their support, assistance, and encouragement during the process of writing this memoir. In no particular order we say thank you and send love and hugs to: The Yoseloff-SABR (Society for American Baseball Research) Baseball Research Grant; John Zajc; Jim Charlton; Andy Hirsch; Rachelle Dang; Annie Inez Logan; George and Elnora Motley; Sam and Patricia Moore; Corky and Mike Stoller; Claudia Lynn and Kermit Don Goree; Loren Mark and Steve Bjerke; Barbara Spranza; Ryan Hallway; Nancy Kauffman DuVall; Cheryl Janis; Andros Sturgeon; Randy Vest; Ann Brigid Clark; Jay Cooper; Gary Mitchem; Carlos "Cuz" Jones; Carl "Mr. Ump" Carlucci; Jeremy Drouin; Malcolm "Jones" Rolsal; Chuck "Tatie Missyelle" Beckett; Scott Riddle; Lanelle Harvey; Blair Harvey; Henry "Bo" Mason; Robert "Bob" Scott; Rick Brown; Kit Kreiger; Ray Doswell; Scott "Feeshla" Fisher; Liz Kenner; Bernice "Sugar Puddin'" Richards; Sean Birdsong; Mary Ross; Ginger Salem; Elle Carriere; Marlene Adler; Ken Burns; Mike Sweeney; Larry Hogan; and Walter Cronkite;

Special thanks to our dear friends Larry Lester and Dionne Warwick for taking time out of your incredibly hectic lives to generously provide us with loving and insightful forewords. We are honored by your friendship and respect.

A huge shout out to Noah Amstadter, John Fishel, and everyone at Sports Publishing, LLC. In particular we acknowledge our brilliant editor, Doug Hoepker, for spearheading this project and all of your tireless work in helping to bring this story to life.

In addition, Byron Motley also acknowledges and thanks: Cocoa Lena who sat at my feet, keeping me company during the countless hours of writing and insisting upon our daily routine of fetch and walks, which enabled my eyeballs much needed relief from the computer screen; all the historians and former players who through the years have helped keep the spirit of the Negro Leagues alive; the music of Chucho Valdés and Burt Bacharach; the silky voices of Azure McCall, Shirley Horne, Leontyne Price, Frederica "Flicka" Von Stade, and of course the voice of life, Dionne Warwick, who all provided a soothing backdrop of wonderful sounds feeding my soul throughout the writing process; my partner Jeff Miiller for meticulously combing through every word of this manuscript, providing invaluable creative ideas helping to make this story even more engaging—*Egészségedre!;* and finally, my treasured friend Gene Davis, who was the first to encourage me to "tell the story," reconnecting me to a deeper, more profound respect for my familial and cultural history. That prompting to embrace Negro League history started me on the journey of a lifetime, and for that I am eternally grateful.

In addition Bob Motley acknowledges: the memories of Uncle Sam Parker and sister Geraldine Motley-Buchanan, who made sure I stayed on the right track.

INDEX

INDEX

INDEX

INDEX